MENTAL HANDICAP: IS ANYTHING WRONG?

THE CARE SERIES

Mental Handicap
Is Anything Wrong?

DAVID C. POTTER

SERIES EDITOR
THE REVD DR NIGEL M DE S CAMERON

KINGSWAY PUBLICATIONS
EASTBOURNE

ISBN 0 86065 988 7

Produced by Bookprint Creative Services
P.O. Box 827, BN23 6NX, England for
KINGSWAY PUBLICATIONS LTD
Lottbridge Drove, Eastbourne, E Sussex BN23 6NT.
Typeset by J&L Composition Ltd, Filey, North Yorkshire
Printed in Great Britain by Clays Ltd, St Ives plc

Introduction to the Series

All around us, Christians are waking up to their responsibility to *care*—for one another, and for all their neighbours in God's world. The old 'social gospel' has been discredited. It tried to rewrite the message and mission of the church as a social and political programme. Many evangelical Christians responded by retreating into a pietism which denied, in effect, that the gospel had social and political implications at all. But more and more they are being called back to their historic role as the heirs of Wilberforce and Shaftesbury. With a fresh confidence in its biblical mandate, the evangelical conscience has reawakened from its fearful slumbers.

Around twenty years ago, two historic developments marked the beginnings of this decisive move towards the recovery of our evangelical heritage. One was the establishment by the Evangelical Alliance of TEAR Fund, to channel evangelical care to needy people overseas. The other was the setting up of the nationwide Festival of Light—now known as CARE (Christian Action, Research and Education)—to channel evangelical concern for the nation. CARE expressed Christian concern through both practical caring initiatives and public, political campaigning.

The roots of CARE's understanding of its mission lie in our stewardship of God's world (which stems from our creation) and our obligations of neighbour-love (underlined anew in Jesus Christ). We have no option but to care for

5

others; and there are two ways in which we may do so—by practical caring for those round about us, and by campaigning for the defence and enhancement of the Christian values of the nation.

This *CARE series* spans these twin concerns. Some books address major public questions, which may be highly controversial. Others focus on practical issues of Christian caring. We pray that this series will help many Christians think through our obligation to be 'salt and light' in society, as loving neighbours and responsible stewards.

NIGEL M DE S CAMERON

Contents

Brothers, think of what you were when you were called. Not many of you were wise by human standards; not many were influential; not many were of noble birth. But God chose the foolish things of the world to shame the wise; God chose the weak things of the world to shame the strong. He chose the lowly things of this world and the despised things—and the things that are not—to nullify the things that are, so that no-one may boast before him.

Paul writing to Christians in Corinth (1 Cor 1:26–29).

"Many a notebook has been filled by people who were moved by the needs they were considering, but who felt neither empowered nor enabled to act in any effective way. We have become used to a certain detachment in the way we approach such things. In fact we have become used to separating knowing from doing. This separation is foreign to the biblical way of thinking."

Roy McCloughry on God's call to Christians to be involved in society. (*The Eye of the Needle* by R. McCloughry, p 160)

"The anguish of people with a handicap reveals our own anguish, their shadows are our shadows, and so we turn away."

Kathryn Spink's summary of Jean Vanier's view of the tension caused by mental handicap. (*Jean Vanier and L'Arche* by Kathryn Spink p 2.)

Preface

This book preaches revolution! Not the revolution of terrorists, anarchists, Marxists and the like. Nor the revolution which tramples the lives of ordinary people in the name of spurious idealism.

It preaches a revolution of attitudes. Its aim is to upset the accepted order of the way most people think about and react to a significant group of people in society.

This book aims to change you. Which begs the question: Do you need to be changed? Maybe, maybe not. Some people who read this book are already revolutionaries—they subscribe to views which are not widely shared by society. They will find themselves in agreement with some or all of what I say. But if most readers reflect the views and attitudes common to our culture they will either reject my thesis or have to change their minds. If their thinking is thus changed their way of life is likely to be affected too!

Revolutions change the way people think *and* talk—and, as those in the know will realise, this book is using language that is in some circles regarded as 'old hat'. The word 'mental' is associated with mental illness and being 'wrong in the head'. The word 'handicap' conjures up pathetic pictures of dependence, of going 'cap in hand' for help. Even government departments no longer use the term 'mental handicap' but instead use 'learning disabilities', which in turn has overtaken the phrase 'learning difficulties'. How, then, do I imagine that I can induce revolution while conforming to the language of the past?

Let me try to explain my position. First, this book is not written for professionals in the field of mental handicap. They may feel that I take shortcuts, that I should deal in more depth with this or that issue, that my application is too personal. To them I say, 'I didn't write this book for you.'

This book has been written for people who are not professionally involved with people with mental handicaps, and perhaps are not in any way, as yet, involved with them. The vast majority of ordinary people do not know that the labels are changing. If I speak about mental handicap they have a rough idea what I am talking about. If I speak about learning disabilities they assume that the topic relates to education. Recently I had a letter from a neighbour of a home for two ladies with severe mental handicaps. She accused a Christian charity of unChristian deception. She had been told that the people who were to move in next door would be people with learning disabilities. 'They don't have learning disabilities,' she wrote. 'They are mentally handicapped.'

Second, the new terms are inadequate as a description of the issue under consideration. Admittedly they don't carry the baggage of prejudice which the old term has, but they include too much. Many people who do not have mental handicaps do have learning disabilities. Those with visual disabilities, with dyslexia, with full or partial deafness, with poor memory, even some very gifted children—these and many more could be included in the designation 'learning disabled'.

Furthermore, learning is only part of the problem. The brain processes the information we acquire, and that function may be impaired even though the learning takes place. Processed information is then put to use, so that we are able to form words, or clean our teeth or whatever. It may be at this point that there is breakdown. So it may reach forwards beyond the learning process to impair the way a person functions.

Third, it would render the title of my book meaningless! It would declare that something is wrong, which would get us off to entirely the wrong start.

Not that I am happy with 'mental handicap' and all the negative attitudes associated with the term. Nor are many of the people so labelled. Having suffered hurt and prejudice some clearly—and understandably—do not want to be referred to in this way. I do wish there was some other term than those which are available at the moment. Those in use at present tend to focus on what people cannot do rather than on what they are and what they can contribute. If only we could find a way of speaking that affirmed people rather than demeaning them. But even if we found the ideal it would still present a problem. Could we ever feel at ease describing over a million people in six or eight syllables, as if they were that much the same as each other?

I want you to be clear of one thing: as used in this book the phrase 'mental handicap' is intended as a term of respect. If it grates with you, I apologise in advance. I also apologise for other terms used in quotations which are far less acceptable today. Oh, and by the way, I am aware of the gender issue too. In no way should what I have written be taken to imply any superiority of men over women in anything!

So, forward to the subject, and 'Long live the revolution'—or, perhaps, 'Short live the revolution!' The sooner people's minds are changed, the better.

Introduction

Tony had a dilemma. A new career offered itself as administrator for a charity providing care for people with mental handicaps. But Tony had a deep-seated fear of disabilities. He knew that it was irrational, but he knew he could not control the wave of anxiety which swept over him whenever he was confronted with people who have handicaps. Could he do the job adequately? Could his fears be overcome?

He decided to face his fears head on by visiting a home run by the charity. He was extremely nervous as he stopped the car outside the house. Bracing himself, he strode to the door and rang the bell. So much hung on what would happen next. The half hour that followed changed his life! He was overwhelmed by the love shown to him by the residents of the home. His fear disappeared for good, indeed he can hardly believe it was ever there. In its place has grown affection and respect for people with all sorts of disabilities.

Tony's fears are common enough and most of us have had a similar anxiety. His new outlook is less common. For most people mental handicap is something they see as 'wrong'.

Is anything wrong?

We know what we mean by 'normal', and we know when something isn't. 'Normal' is right; the other is wrong. Somehow. But how?

The child, unable to talk, communicates its pleasure by smiles and touches. The young man cannot read but spends hours looking at beautiful books. The woman cannot sing but listens spellbound to lovely music. A person who has never cooked a meal for herself draws silken pictures with a needle. One child grows up and leaves home to carve out a career, marry and begin a family. Another stays at home. One son succeeds in everything he does; his brother does very little.

Is anything wrong? It depends where you start from. A few miles from where I live stands a grand Victorian mansion. It is set in hundreds of acres of rolling parkland, far away from crowds and communities and bus routes. This tranquil location has been home for hundreds of people who live in the buildings in the grounds. They too have mental handicaps and also need staff to care for them. They are set apart from society because something is wrong. But with what, with whom?

Previous generations answered with confidence: 'They are not normal. They are better off with their own kind. They will be happier away from the bustle of the town.' In this way fear and prejudice were clothed with a mantle of concern.

We visited a house where three young(ish) men lived together. They welcomed us as old friends—which we are—and showed us round their home. Our attention was drawn to the new lampshades, the TV in the lounge and, in particular, to the room of the person who was our guide. An ordinary thing to happen on the first visit to friends who have recently moved into a new house. It so happens that the three men need help to live there because each of them has a mental handicap. Staff are employed to give that help. Is there anything wrong with that?

Some people think that there is a great deal wrong. Two women with mental handicaps were cared for in an ordinary house on an estate which, when it was built, was the biggest in Europe. Just one house with two residents among thousands of dwellings and dwellers. Again, staff were needed to help them cope with things they could not do for themselves. The neighbours scowled, complained, protested. One couple paid their solicitor to write a hostile letter. Something must be wrong! With what? With whom?

Is anything wrong? Obviously! There is something terribly wrong if people who must depend on others, for no fault of their own, are made outcasts by their own communities. Today mental handicap hospitals are closing and the residents are moving into the community by government decree. But the community is not always welcoming. Civilisation has not necessarily made us more civil!

What is wrong is the attitude which refuses to face the enormous diversity in the human race. What's wrong are systems—in health, education, social standards, and so on—which reinforce those attitudes and banish people from the bosom of the community because they do not or cannot conform to a narrow definition of what is OK.

Mental handicap keeps cropping up in the news. Just occasionally it is good news—the first girl with Down's syndrome to win the coveted Duke of Edinburgh's gold award. A mentally handicapped child joins the cast of a TV soap opera. A young couple with mental handicaps perform a moving dance on a TV talent show. Lovely, bright spots on an otherwise gloomy scene.

For most of the time the media portray the most depressing picture of people with mental handicaps. There was the case of the young woman with a mental handicap whose mother wanted her to be sterilised to prevent her becoming pregnant. The case went to the House of Lords for a ruling, but on the way the publicity it received underlined the low regard of society for people with handicaps. Almost no one seemed to see the frightening implications of enforced surgery; the reason is that people failed to see the young woman as like themselves.

A few years earlier there was the trial of a doctor who allowed a baby with Down's syndrome to die. He was acquitted of murder after the universally negative testimony of medical experts concerning children with this condition.

Then there were the debates in Parliament in the late 80s and 1990 concerning abortion. A major concern of MPs was to prevent the birth of babies with handicaps. Along with the debates on research on human embryos, the elimination of handicaps and disabilities seemed to be the most desirable objective.

Something seems to be wrong

For my part, I refuse to be depressed about mental handicap. This will not be a depressing book either. Its simple thesis is this: Yes, there is something wrong—with attitudes towards people with mental handicaps. If these attitudes can be changed then we are all in for a better time.

Christians are as much a part of society as other people, with attitudes as much affected by the popular outlook. We are as likely to admire the 'cult of cleverness' because it is the air we breathe in our Western culture. We have to step back to view our own landscape and ask if what we see reflects what the Bible teaches. The life and ministry of Jesus presents us with the challenge to live differently by a better standard to a more meaningful end. It is an exciting challenge and our response to it will affect the lives of other people—some of whom may have a mental handicap.

You will always have the poor with you, Jesus said. As things stand you will have people with mental handicaps too. That you cannot change, apart from genocide. But attitudes can be changed. Then behaviour will be changed. And, as most people with mental handicaps are now living with their families in the community, then society has the potential to be greatly enriched!

I

What's the Problem?

Pardon?
  I asked, 'What's the problem?'
  Well, it's obvious, isn't it? Mental handicap is the problem. That's what this book is about, so that's got to be the problem.
  Well, I still have to ask the same question: 'What's the problem?'
  Look, there are at least one million people in Britain who have a mental handicap. That's got to be a problem. It's a problem for education. Children with this sort of disability find it harder to learn, so they need special schools. It's a problem for the health services. Mental handicap is often associated with physical problems—heart condition, vulnerability to infection, epilepsy, allergy to certain drugs, and so on. It's a problem for society. More money has to be found for these extra services. And then they have to be cared for when parents can't or won't cope. More taxes have to be raised. And you ask, 'What's the problem?'!
  I see all of that. But doesn't it depend on how you look at things? Remember those scorching summers in 1989 and 1990 in the South of England. Fabulous weather week after week with hot sunshine blazing from a clear blue sky. So different from what we are used to that we hardly knew what to talk about. We had frequent barbecues in the garden. Sales of air conditioners shot up. We could have beautiful suntan without going to the Med. Wonderful stuff—for some of us.

For others it was a mammoth problem. Farmers watched fields of vegetables shrivel in the baked earth. Water authorities fretted at falling water levels in their reservoirs. Transport departments worried about melting road surfaces. Even railway lines buckled.

Was the weather a problem or not? Your answer will depend largely on how it affected you. The long hours of hot sunshine were not, I suggest, the problem. If they were, life in the tropics must be one long problem! Rather it was the unreadiness of our infrastructure to cope with such temperatures that resulted in so many difficulties.

What has all this to do with the problem of mental handicap?

There you go again, calling it a problem. Although mental handicap raises a number of important issues, it is no more of a problem than the weather.

And where does that lead us?

To this—that we can begin to consider mental handicap positively rather than negatively.

But you can't just sidestep the issues I raised earlier. What about the educational issues? What about the health services required? What about the cost of long-term care and all the other consequences we could mention? If we don't need to provide the extras let's say so and stop them as soon as possible!

Can we just agree another starting point. Other things will follow in due course. As long as you insist on seeing mental handicap as a problem you will also see the person with a mental handicap as a problem. Is it fair to discount one million fellow citizens in this way? Let's drop the notion that mental handicap is a problem and see whether, from a different perspective, the view will be different too.

Differentness

We expect people to be different. Imagine how you would feel on entering a room full of people who looked exactly alike. It's the stuff nightmares are made of; we would react strongly against something so unnatural. Given that there are differences between the sexes, we are accustomed to seeing tremendous variety among groups of people. And that variety is something we actually cultivate. Most of us look for clothes which will enhance our distinctiveness—even if we are not very distinctive.

God seems extravagant when you look at creation, for no two things are exactly alike; similar maybe, but different too. Small wonder therefore that we see that differentness carried to almost infinite lengths in human beings. Culture and colour, knowledge and wisdom, wealth and poverty, art and utility, height and weight, language and literature—about the only thing common to us all is that we are all different.

But, for reasons that are hard to find, when we face the issue of mental handicap this basic assumption seems to evaporate. We tend to talk of 'the mentally handicapped', as if they were all the same, all one million of them. And they aren't. There is no more reason to describe people with a mental handicap as identical than any other group of people. They are different from one another—in ability, in interest, in size, in taste, in temperament, and so on. And they are more like everyone else than they are different from them.

Normal or not?

All right, I follow the argument so far, but it doesn't help too much because we all know what is normal. And you surely aren't trying to say that mentally handicapped people are normal? If that was the case we would never have labelled them.

Now there's an interesting thought. What do you mean by normal? It is now normal for British homes to have a washing machine, refrigerator, vacuum cleaner and colour television. Forty years ago it was the province of the rich to own such luxury items. It is now normal to see people of all classes wearing denim, though its first introduction was exclusive to 'scruffy' young people. It is now normal to leave school with some form of qualification, though many people who are now retiring never sat an examination in their lives. What does all this show? That normality is not a fixed standard, a rule we can use at all times and in all places to measure what is right and not right.

The same thing holds true in more personal matters and we learn to cope with it on a daily basis. Some of us are tall and some are short. The fact that a friend is one or other does not determine our regard for him. If he is exceptionally tall—or short—we may be embarrassed to look up—or down—at him. We might be self-conscious to walk into town in his company. But we would never say that his height—or lack of it—is something *wrong*. Just different. Different from what we regard as usual—or normal.

This point is so important to the way we think about handicap and disability that we must take it a little further still. Take a look at education, and in particular special education.

Special education facilities have been created in response to the definition of certain categories of children as not fitting 'normal' categories.[1]

But are there not tests which can show whether or not a child is of normal intelligence? The tests rest upon the assumptions that are themselves problematic. 'Tests measure what tests measure and nothing else.'[2]

The mention of IQ tests may bring us a step closer to understanding our dilemma. Let us assume for the moment that the tests prove something. The majority of people in Britain are probably in the IQ range 90 to 110, with 100 being average. Someone with an IQ of 140 is above average; someone with a score of 70 is below average. All that has been shown is what is usual in our Western European society. The same tests used in West Africa or Northern India or South America would show different results—indeed this has been true within Britain to the disadvantage of ethnic groups.

Do you see where this is leading us? The threshold of our

difficulty with mental handicap is not 'out there' somewhere. It is within us. Because we regard what is average as 'normal' and what is 'normal' as OK, we reject what is not average as being not 'normal'. If we could stretch our own boundaries of normality we would include some who are not average as also OK—perhaps some who have mental handicaps. If we accept as 'normal' something which is found in every country, in every racial, social or language group, then mental handicap must be included. If we accept as 'normal' something which has been part of human history almost from the beginning, then mental handicap must be included.

As Brian Stratford said about one form of mental handicap:

> . . . the absolute beginning of Down's syndrome would be with Genesis, the creation of human life, and would begin when people started to multiply. Down's syndrome is therefore not a disease, it is part of our rich and varied biological inheritance.[3]

The same could be said of mental handicap as a whole.

At this point there is a danger that we may be misunderstood. We are not saying that mental handicap does not exist. That would require a massive act of self-deception which could not be sustained. Rather we are saying that people should be accepted on the basis that they are people, not because they are average. That way we can cope with the enormous diversity of people among whom we live in our communities. The fact that some are not average will not then result in our discriminating against them. The majority in our community may be 'whites', but that does not make 'blacks' non-normal. The majority may be agnostics, but that does not make Christians non-normal. The majority may have average intelligence, but that does not make people with mental handicaps non-normal.

Fear

The most common reaction to people with mental handicaps is fear. And fear is a catalyst for prejudice. The fear may be born of ignorance—of not knowing what mental handicap is or how it affects a person. 'Will he understand me if I talk to him?' 'What if I can't understand what he says?' 'How will I cope if he does something strange?'

Ignorance is further exaggerated by the folklore of mental handicap, the stories and rumours which reinforce concern and feed anxiety. This has more to do with the past than with the present, the legacy of 150 years of segregating people with mental handicaps from the rest of the community.

Fear has been reinforced by the media and assisted by the authorities. Back in 1981/82 the middle-class holiday resort of Teignmouth leapt into the headlines because some of its hoteliers refused to accept people with a mental handicap. Local councillors made a political issue of it, promising to rid the town of 'the mentally handicapped menace'. There was an outcry at such a scandalous attitude by the comfortable elderly population of the resort. What was not publicised was that the furore was sparked by a group of fifty to sixty people on holiday from a mental handicap hospital, inadequately staffed, dressed institutionally, displaying highly unsocial behaviour, led around in hand-holding, zombie-like crocodiles. The blame for their rejection by the hoteliers and burghers of Teignmouth must be shared by the hospital authorities which sent them on holiday so hopelessly equipped for the world outside the institution.

Nor is Parliament free from fear and prejudice as far as mental handicap is concerned. In 1990 the Human Fertilisation and Embryo Bill passed through both Houses to receive the royal assent. There is much within the Act to disturb the thoughtful person, not least the attitude manifested towards people with physical disabilities or mental handicaps. It is betrayed in the permissive nature of the section on abortion. A baby thought to be healthy may not be aborted after twenty-four weeks of pregnancy. A baby thought to have a disability or mental handicap can be aborted at any time up to the moment of birth. The debate revealed that, for a large majority of Parliamentarians, disability or mental handicap is unacceptable. The baby is better off dead!

From fear to prejudice

At the risk of labouring the point, it is important to show that prejudice is real towards people with mental handicaps. It is not a figment of paranoid imaginations. It shows itself in a number of ways.

Housing for instance. All of us need somewhere to live and assume the right to choose where and how, within the means available to us. As things stand if you, as a nurse, say, or a student, or a mechanic, wanted to share a house with five other friends or colleagues that would be permissible. If you chose to have seven children and to live together as a single family—perhaps importing Grandma to help—there is no legislation to curb your freedom. Suppose, however, that you are one of a group of six people with mental handicaps who want to share a house together with the support of visiting staff. You will have some hurdles to leap before you can do so. First you will need planning consent. Then you will need to register the 'home' with the local authority. Before they will agree to that you will have to precautions against fire, which is certain to include a fire escape, fire exit signs, extinguishers and alarm bells. And this in turn will create a reaction from the neighbourhood!

A Cause for Concern was offered a lovely house in Deganwy. The owners were so impressed with the charity's work in caring for adults with mental handicaps that they decided to sell their home to the charity for half its market value. The sale went ahead. Then came the planning application. Believing it to be fair to inform the neighbours before the event, the charity invited them to a meeting to tell them of their plans. The church hall was packed, the atmosphere tense and the opposition total. The local councillors joined in the opposition. The planning application was turned down for reasons the charity considered inadequate. They appealed against the refusal and consent was given for the project to proceed. (Some neighbours wrote subsequently to withdraw their opposition and express their support for the home.)

A project in Haywards Heath was halted by a neighbour who gazumped the charity, buying the house with cash—and then erecting other dwellings in the garden. A resident living opposite a house where a home was to open put his own house on the market the day planning consent was granted. After public hostility to a small group of people with mental handicaps living in Alton, the authorities closed the home and moved the residents elsewhere. It happened in Woodley too. And elsewhere, again and again and again.

This sort of opposition comes from all social groups, but is more evident in well-heeled districts. Research shows that reasons given fall into one of five categories:

1 the value of neighbouring property will fall, a fact which is not supported by such research as has taken place;
2 that residents will behave in an unacceptable manner, even though those who live in the house may be unknown to the protesters;
3 that there will be a high level of noise, though from what or who is uncertain, and it is unlikely to exceed that of other (young) people;
4 that children will be at risk, usually because of the assumed lack of sexual restraint alleged to be common to people with mental handicaps;
5 that extra traffic will be generated.[4]

Such objections relate to folklore rather than the facts.

At the time of writing it is increasingly hard to obtain dental treatment paid for in full by the National Health Service. For people with only a 'pocket money' income this is very difficult. Many people with mental handicaps find that they are refused treatment for financial reasons; many more are refused on the grounds that the dental surgeon does not provide a 'specialist service'. What they need is someone to attend to their teeth, and teeth are teeth no matter in whose mouth they are found!

A similar reluctance is sometimes expressed by General Practitioners asked to take on a patient with a mental handicap. Treatments are sometimes refused on the grounds that the person has a mental handicap. Even as I write I have learned of a young man refused treatment for a serious kidney condition on the grounds that he is non-urgent due to his mental handicap. The intervention of a Christian doctor ensured that treatment was given, but not soon enough to save his life.

Is this really the tip of the iceberg? Perhaps so. Maurice, a man with a mental handicap, was taken ill on Christmas Day with acute stomach pains. The doctor who was called was not his usual GP. He left saying that Maurice's only problem was that he was drunk, and he had better not be called again. The next day Maurice was admitted to hospital with a burst appendix.

Peter Morgan had a heart defect—a fairly common consequence of Down's syndrome. The consultant explained to Peter's mother that 'while some hospitals operated according to need, others had restricted lists, because of costs, and therefore gave priority to normal and younger people, while a third group declined to operate on the handicapped'.[5]

On the receiving end—the family

To learn that your newborn baby has a mental handicap is both shocking and disorientating. The way in which the information is given to the parents will contribute to how they react to such unwelcome news. But even the gentlest approach will leave parents at best bewildered and at worst distraught.

We regard ourselves as fortunate in the doctor and nurse who cared for Madeleine when our daughter Rachel was born. The birth took place at home, and I was present. It had been a long and difficult labour and when the baby finally eased herself into the world the nurse wrapped her in a towel and thrust her at me. Madeleine needed urgent attention.

I looked down at this strange, tiny bundle in my arms. Her face was smeared with blood and she looked blue, as if with cold. The word that popped into my mind was 'mongol', but she was our first child and I had never before seen a newborn baby. Later the doctor and nurse talked in hushed tones and at length by the front door. Was I right?

Rachel was a winner. She was a lovely baby and a real joy to us. My first suspicions were soon forgotten and never shared with Madeleine. Weeks slipped by and Rachel put on weight. However, she was troubled by a persistent tummy upset so I rang the doctor. He asked me to visit him at the end of surgery that evening. He gently explained that Rachel had a handicap and that it would become increasingly evident as she grew older. It was only when I asked if there was some name by which the condition was known that he used the then common term 'mongolism'.

Not all parents are dealt with so kindly. One mother asked the nurse why she couldn't have her baby by her as other mothers in the ward had theirs. The nurse replied, 'You'd better get used to the idea that your baby's not normal.' Many parents feel resentment at the way they were informed. A pastor rang to ask for help in respect of a young couple in his church. They had just been told that their baby boy had Down's syndrome. The pediatrician wanted to know whether or not the parents wanted him to live. The pastor asked for advice on what to say to the parents. Sometimes parents are bewildered by the unexplained difference in routine with their newborn baby. It is whisked away from the labour ward to the Special Care Unit. Blood tests are taken from child and mother. Consultants look serious as they ask veiled questions about family history.

Several studies on the problem of telling parents the diagnosis of Down's syndrome have reported complaints by parents that they were not told together, in a sensitive way, that they were not told soon enough, that they were told in front of a large number of people and no privacy was available, that the baby was not present, that they were not given any or enough information, and that they had no further support or time to work through their reactions and feelings.[6]

Conditions which are identified at birth necessitate that parents are informed gently and sensitively of the facts. They have anticipated this birth for many months. The longed-for child already has a personality in their imagination. They have probably dreamed of a beautiful daughter or clever son who will be an extension of themselves without their own warts! Suddenly to be told that these things may not be can prove devastating. To be offered the opportunity to decide whether or not the real child should live or die is an intolerable burden at a time when parents are ill-equipped to cope with the news, let alone the decision.

Positive previous experience of a person with mental handicap will help parents to make a positive response. Hazel Morgan was encouraged by the story of Norman she had learned from her grandmother. He was the vicar's son whom Hazel met once or twice and found to be a delightful man with Down's syndrome. It served to help her when she learned that her second son had the same condition.

For some parents the realisation that something is different dawns more slowly. It may be months before someone will listen to their concern that the child is not developing as expected. Of course parents may be needlessly anxious, and many doubtless are. But it is a fearfully isolating experience for a mother to find professional backs turned towards her worried enquiries.

One mother wrote feelingfully of her experience in this regard:

It is, to my mind, one of the most exquisitely cruel aspects of early childhood autism that it only becomes apparent to the parents very slowly that there is anything wrong with the child.
    Simon, from the moment he was put into my arms after his birth, was pink, and smooth, and perfect, so perfect that all the

anxieties of pregnancy fell away at once, and I smiled at my own stupidity. Of course he was beautiful. I was not physically deformed, and I was married to a healthy good-looking man. I had every right to expect so marvellous a baby.[7]

It was four years before Simon was finally diagnosed as having autism.

Madeleine burst into tears as she closed the front door behind her. She had just returned from a visit to the Medical Officer of Health with Rachel, now two years old. 'Put her in a home and forget you ever had her,' was his advice. That was in 1965 and, thankfully, such advice is less common today. And the institutions are less readily available.

The medical profession is in an unenviable position. Doctors and nurses are not exempt from the fears and prejudices which affect society in general. They are trained to meet everybody's expectation of health and happiness. They are committed to making ill people well and weak people strong. Permanent, irreversible disability presents them with a dilemma. It is not a disease and cannot be cured, so what should be done with it?

The parents of a child with a mental handicap may well experience something akin to bereavement when they learn of the disability of their child. That dreamed of, longed for child has died. This baby with a mental handicap is not the child they had prepared for and anticipated with such excitement. Their hopes lie in tatters at their feet. It is not uncommon for parents to choose a different name for the child rather than use the one they had planned for a 'normal' child. Perhaps they can use it for one they might bear later. Until this real loss is faced and come to terms with the process of acceptance cannot begin.

Becoming a parent is quite an experience—and not necessarily easier because it has happened before. Parenting is one of the most important jobs in life, but we are not usually given the chance to practice! Suddenly a tiny, helpless life is *our* responsibility, totally. Mess this up and the results will last a lifetime! (Why are we so keen to try our hand?)

How much more insecure and vulnerable parents will feel if this little bundle of being has a disability. What should they expect of it? What allowances should they make for the mental handicap? How will they know if things are going wrong? Who can advise them? It is an awesome prospect and one on which there is barely time to reflect. There is so much to be done for the baby while at the same time struggling with one's fears and emotions—not to mention the reactions of the wider family, friends and neighbours. Grandparents, for example, often find it more difficult to come to terms with than the parents themselves.

Then there are the brothers and sisters. This more dependent person will inevitably absorb more time—more clinics, more hospital visits, more nappies for more years, and so on. Parents may justifiably feel that the whole family is handicapped by the experience.

Wisely handled, however, the presence of a person with a mental handicap in a family can be very much to the good of other children. Their ability to accept and respond to other people with disabilities and handicaps will be developed. It is notable that one meets a number of siblings of mentally handicapped people within the caring professions!

The whole family may find itself on the receiving end of attitudes which bring pain and sadness. Miriam was arguing vigorously with Anna outside the bathroom door. They were only ten years of age, but play had given place to a full-scale row. Madeleine went to investigate. Anna, a frequent visitor, had that day learned that Rachel was thirteen years old. She couldn't cope with the discovery that someone she had previously accepted as much like herself was so much older. She had shut Rachel in the bathroom!

These are real issues. Thankfully they are not universal, nor is the task of caring for a mentally handicapped person permanently negative. Within the medical profession there are those who are outstanding in the help and care they provide. Some parents find themselves overwhelmed by the assistance offered. There are those in the church and community who are welcoming and supportive. There are officials in social services departments and education departments who could not be more helpful. There are children who accept another child with a mental handicap with no reserve. But what I have described briefly are real experiences with which most families with a mentally handicapped person will relate. As they say, exceptions prove the rule. The fact that someone is treated positively becomes a matter for comment.

Some years ago an interesting and revealing study of attitudes towards people with mental handicaps was undertaken in two villages in Israel. Sixty-six per cent thought there should be no contact between mentally handicapped people and children. Sixty-eight per cent thought people with mental handicaps should be allowed to work, but in special workshops. Ninety-five per cent thought that people with mental handicaps should live in institutions. In spite of this, young men living in a mental handicap institution were invited to help out at harvest time. They picked oranges with care and enthusiasm, ate in the homes of the villagers and played with local children. After the harvest was over a second survey measured how attitudes had changed. The survey found that people held exactly the same views as previously, 'But please,' they asked, 'send those nice young men back here again next year'![8] A curious story, which at least shows that the idea of mental handicap is less acceptable than the person with a mental handicap.

Salute to the brave

What is it like for the person with a mental handicap? Here we have a problem. We can find out what parents feel from the numerous books written by mothers and fathers about their experience of bringing up a child with a mental handicap. We can find out what people with physical disabilities feel about themselves and the way they are treated by other people either by asking them or by reading books written by those with first-hand experience. But, by the nature of the case, similar information about the feelings of people with mental handicaps is harder to come by. Even the self-advocacy movement can only give the subjective perspectives of individuals with mental handicap.

That may be how it appears at first glance. By listening to the words and ways of individuals with mental handicaps one is able to piece together a fairly accurate picture of how they feel about themselves and the way they are treated by society. This will reveal the widely varied experience of each person, but there will be some common themes which are less than encouraging.

Hazel Morgan, in *Through Peter's Eyes*, imagines her son who has Down's syndrome asking himself the question 'Are they pleased with me?' The question is imagined in the context of the child being held by his mother, prodded by doctors and gazed upon by a sad-faced father. Who knows what the newborn understands of acceptance or non-acceptance at this stage of life, except that it is reasonable to suppose an emotional response to the warmth or otherwise of its welcome into the world.

You won't read far in books on mental handicap without coming across a quotation from or reference to the writings of Jean Vanier. Reflecting upon the reactions of parents facing the fact of mental handicap in their child, he takes the issue further.

All these sufferings deeply affect the child. It is a terrible thing for a child to feel it has let its parents down and is the cause of their pain and tears. The wounded hearts of parents wound the heart of the child. A healthy child senses itself as the cause of joy and the centre of delighted attention, one whom everyone wants to touch, to hug and to hold. . . .

Sometimes I am asked: 'Is a child or an adult who has a severe mental handicap aware of his or her condition? Do they suffer from this?' For the most part, I don't know. But this I do know: the tiniest infant senses if it is loved and wanted, or not. Similarly, people with a mental handicap, even a severe one, sense immediately whether they are loved and valued by the way they are looked at, spoken to and welcomed. A baby who has a mental handicap, sensing that it is not wanted, will harden its heart and body and, to protect itself, will withdraw from reality. There is thus a sort of inner death.[9]

Roger Meyers, a mentally handicapped man who fought the system to hold down a job, marry his girlfriend and live in a home of their own, wrote a poem about his experience. It begins like this: 'Someone being slow, they are way down low.'[10]. That was how he read his position in the esteem of others. And among adults with mental handicaps this lack of self-worth is a common feature.

Where does it come from? Is it an essential, inevitable part of their mental handicap, a result of not being able to learn properly? No. In fact they have learned well enough to know the reactions and attitudes of other people towards them. As little children they were scooped off to a different type of education—'special' it was called. Segregated from their brothers and sisters, they met up with children whom they never met on their own street, whom they could not easily visit for play and companionship. They shared the campus with similarly handicapped children and young people from the age of two and a half years to nineteen, never changing schools unless they moved to another town.

Then on leaving school little consideration was given to their aspirations for a career or work. They were sent to a centre specialised in keeping them occupied. Perhaps there were some light industrial processes or packaging, and outings for swimming and horse riding. There may even have been an attempt to train them in independent living skills. All through the message being fed to them is the same— you are unacceptably different. And that differentness was institutionalised by the way the state provided for them.

Rejection is also commonplace at the hands of people in the community. The next-door neighbour was heard scolding her child: 'I told you not to play with her. You might catch something. She's not normal.' Other children may be heard laughing at the person with a mental handicap or calling that person names. The school bus may have been stoned as it passed the comprehensive school entrance.

Daily life experience for a mentally handicapped person involves subtle and overt discrimination in shops, on buses, in the street, and even in church. The last is particularly sad, and more common than one might expect. Groups attending the service from hostels or even Christian homes have been known to be asked not to come again. The ability to sing in tune is obviously an essential qualification for heaven!

It would not be surprising to find that the people who are treated in this way had given up on life, if they showed no interest in other people, gave no care to their own appearance and simply withdrew from life around them. Many do so, particularly those who have spent much of their life in institutions. More react as if challenging a system which seeks to degrade them. John and Gerald dress smartly if a special visitor is expected. Evelyn can be relied on to engage the stranger in conversation. Kate, too, will want to discuss issues with the visitor. Linda will provide as warm a welcome as he or she has ever received. Mark's face will say all it can to express delight at meeting an old friend. Forgiving of the system which discriminates against them, of a society which rejects them, in spite of deep wounds, many hold tenaciously to their fragile self-respect and vulnerable security.

There are, inevitably, many frustrations and disappointments for a person with a mental handicap. Increasingly their disability is described as a learning difficulty, and it includes that. They struggle to learn information and skills many of us absorb without effort. But it is also more than that, for they are frequently limited in how they use what they have learned. Many of our friends have superb memories, recalling events, places and people from years ago; reciting information acquired long before. Whenever I meet Andrew he will remind me of something which happened when he came to

our home in about 1979. 'David Potter. Telly not working!'
He remembers my embarrassment and teases me still.

Learning information is one thing. Processing it and putting
it to effective use is something different. Skills that are
learned in one setting frequently do not transfer to another
for the person with a mental handicap. To be able to cook
an omelette in your kitchen will not guarantee that Mary will
be able to cook an omelette in my kitchen!

Seeing that their lives are different from their peers',
especially their own brothers' and sisters', is bound to shadow
their enjoyment of life. For some it will be a sadness that is
absorbed and unexpressed. For some it will result in behaviour
which is disruptive. Even the most severely handicapped
person is by no means devoid of either sense or feeling!

All of which is written as a salute to the brave, rather than
to engender sentimentalism or sympathy. We do well to
respect those who bear disadvantages most of us would find
utterly crushing.

Receiving in reverse

It is a curious thing that if you talk to people who live and
work with individuals with mental handicaps you will frequently
find them very positive about those for whom they care. They
will speak with warmth and even enthusiasm about those
individuals whom others disregard. That is not what you
might expect. They will be realistic about the aggression, or
tears, or mind-bending repetition, but as well as that they
will express their admiration for the sheer character and
personal strength of people with mental handicaps.

Talk to the parent of a child with Down's syndrome who
has just started to walk, perhaps a whole year after other
children of similar age. She will be over the moon. Talk to
a care assistant who has just helped a teenager to feed himself
with a spoonful of food for the very first time. His joy will
be unbounded. Speak to a speech therapist who has just
heard the first full sentence from a man with mental handicap

who a few months ago hardly said anything. Doubling her salary would not give her as much pleasure.

Why is it? It cannot be sentiment—that is too fragile to bear the weight of living with disadvantage and handicap. Perhaps it is that those who share some or all of their lives with mentally handicapped people actually receive something from them, see more than is easily observed by those whose eyes hold fear and whose lives are too busy for the slower pace.

The quality of friendship, of real loyalty, given to us by people with mental handicaps is precious, unequalled among other friends. The unconditional acceptance they offer has restored confidence and hope to many who have lived and worked with them. The patience with which Mark repeats what he is saying so that I can understand him, and the way he congratulates me when at last I have understood, is humbling. The perseverance of Clive is amazing when there is something his brain wants to communicate and his body wants to stifle.

Evidently many people find this hard to cope with so they attribute the credit to the person who provides the care rather than to the person about whom they speak. We admire the carer for qualities we regard as special, and we conclude that this is not a job for ordinary people! We are reluctant to face the possibility that there is more to be discovered about people with mental handicaps than we realised.

This is the testimony of Jean Vanier:

> When I started to live with men and women who were more or less disfigured, I wanted to give them a human face. In so doing I discovered that it was they who gave a human face to me.[11]

There is something to be received by all of us from the people with mental handicaps who are living nearby, whose contribution is not available to us because of our fears and prejudices. There is beauty to be seen which may cut right across our usual expectations of prettiness but lie deep within a character. There are qualities to be experienced which our bustling world has devalued.

Where do we go from here? Back to basics! Before we can make any progress in understanding we need to be sure on one fundamental issue.

Notes

[1] P. Squibb, *Special Education: Policy, Practices and Social Issues* (Harper & Row: London, 1981), p 42.

[2] *Ibid*, pp 43–44.

[3] B. Stratford, *Down's Syndrome: Past, Present and Future* (Penguin: London, 1989), p xiii.

[4] P. Roycroft and A. Hames, 'Local Objections to Community-based Houses for People with Mental Handicaps', *Mental Handicap*, vol 18 (March 1991): p 11.

[5] H. Morgan, *Through Peter's Eyes* (Arthur James: London, 1990), pp 41–42.

[6] C. Cunningham and H. Davis, in M. Craft, J. Bicknell and S. Hollins (eds), *Mental Handicap* (Balliere Tindall: London, 1985), p 162.

[7] A. Lovell, *Simple Simon* (Lion: Tring, 1978), pp 1–2.

[8] A. Wynn-Jones, 'The Teignmouth Syndrome', *Community Care* (21 August 1986): p 18.

[9] J. Vanier, *Man and Woman He Made Them* (Darton, Longman & Todd: London, 1984), pp 12, 14.

[10] Quoted in P. Gilbert, *Mental Handicap: A Practical Guide for Social Workers* (BPI: London, 1985), p 13.

[11] Vanier, *op cit*, p 2.

2

What's the Likeness?

Our mental and emotional focus seems geared to notice difference more readily than similarity. It is as if we have some internal mechanism which registers when something varies from an invisible standard, or some antennae which pick up irregularities on our way. So our natural inclination at this point is to examine what is different about people with mental handicaps. To do that now would be to make a colossal presupposition. It would assume what the standard is without considering what it might or should be. It would evade a much more basic issue which will prove crucial to everything else which follows in this book, and will determine our attitudes to people with mental handicaps.

The fundamental question to be faced is: What makes people, people? What is it that marks out the human race from every other form of life on this crowded planet of ours? It is an ancient question, asked by philosophers from before Greece was an empire, but it is arguably one of the most pressing questions for today as well—*What is man*?

Finding an answer is important today because there are moral issues which face us frequently which can only be properly resolved if we have found out what man is. When over twenty-five million people were facing famine in Africa in 1991 there seemed no time to ask about philosophy. Action was needed. So they showed scenes on our television screens of pot-bellied children staggering about on spindle-like legs and hopeless, despairing mothers by newly dug graves. But somehow it was unreal, almost as if these were not people at all! And then there were the terrible conditions of Kurds in Northern Iraq, and devastating floods in Bangladesh—all happening at more or less the same time. Then came Bosnia Herzegovena. The aid agencies pleaded with us for pity and the media wrote about compassion fatigue. Did we feel any obligation towards these ragged, alien beings? Were they really people like us?

Abortion has been to the fore of public debate in recent years in Britain. Euthanasia is increasingly receiving mention and has been raised yet again in Parliament. The debates tend to focus either on particularly harrowing examples— real or hypothetical —and on rights. After all a fetus sounds inhuman; an old man who dribbles and has lost his memory seems to have become less than a man. Are they really people like us?

Perhaps our problem is that we don't know how to solve the riddle, or where to look for an answer to the question. We will hardly dare ask who we are, let alone what we are! Life is too pressing for such speculation. There is a living to be earned, a mortgage to pay, a youth group to organise, a sermon to preach, the shopping to be done. And, anyway, this book is supposed to be about mental handicap so let's get on with it! Which is exactly the point I want to make. If we know what it is that qualifies a person to be included in the human race then we can discover if people with mental handicaps are so qualified. If they are, we have to look at how we encourage that to be the case for people in our own community. If they are not, we will then be able to legitimise their segregation.

An organising principle

Where shall we begin in our search for an answer to such a vital question? What we need is some means by which all the parts of the issue can be addressed, a principle which can

be applied in a wide variety of different situations—an organising principle. This principle has to stand three tests:
—Does it include everything that needs to be included?
—Does it exclude everything which does not fit the criteria?
—Is it universally true?

The organising principle we seek must include every human being, so it has to relate to men and women, girls and boys, old and young, rich and poor, tall and short, fat and thin, every colour and skin shade, every religion, philosophy and creed.

The principle must also exclude whatever is not really human—animals which may look something like us, birds that talk, dogs that fetch newspapers, creatures that walk upright on two legs. Without demeaning them in any way, the principle must show them to be not human and thus to give them a different place in the scheme of things.

And the principle must be universally true. Whether it is applied to Tamils in India or Aucas in the Amazon; whether it describes Englishmen in France or Russians visiting Disneyland; the principle must be as relevant to the one as to the other. It must always be true too. It must be meaningful whether we are discussing people living tens of thousands of years before or after us. We cannot risk a principle which might have changed or ceased to apply one morning as we stumble out into the world.

All we have to do is find the principle! Believe me, it is essential that we do so, even if we have to fumble with unfamiliar philosophy or theology. It is the one sure way of finding a sound footing for our understanding of mental handicap. It is the only route to deciding a realistic response to it. So 'hang in there'—and I will make it as interesting as I can.

When I said earlier that the question 'What is man?' has been asked by philosophers and religious teachers for hundreds upon hundreds of years, I did not intend to imply that no one has found any answers! In fact the options for an organising principle are legion. Every major (and minor) religion presents its credentials. Every major (and minor) philosopher will join the queue to offer a solution. But the primary focus of this book is not philosophy.

At this point I have to exercise some self-control. Others have discussed the possibilities in detail and there is no need to repeat their efforts. I would enjoy comparing and contrasting the distinctly different principles put forward by secular humanism and Christianity, for example. Two things deter me. First, such a comparison has already been written brilliantly by others, notably Jim Packer in *Christianity: the True Humanism*. Second, our focus is much narrower in that we want to know whether there is a valid organising principle which explains who we are and embraces people with mental handicap. And in line with the purpose of this book we must enquire whether Christian doctrine can provide such a principle.

A Christian organising principle

There is no room for favouritism here. Christianity must produce a principle which meets in full the expectations that we seek. It must fit the way things are *and* the way we feel about them. We feel ourselves to be significant as human beings in a way animals are not—no disrespect to the cat! We feel that the real self is more than the body in which we live, that we are not simply some sort of biological machine. The principle must also take account of our awareness of the divine, indeed it cannot fail to do so.

> A doctrine of man which tries to deal with man in separation from God has committed an error which will distort every truth which it discovers.[1]

The answer to the question 'What is man?' begins to be unravelled in the opening chapter of the Bible. Genesis chapter 1 describes to us the drama of creation and takes us to the point where the major work has been done. One thing more remained to be achieved—and we are given a glimpse of God making a strategic decision.

> Then God said, 'Let us make man in our image, in our likeness, and let them rule over the fish of the sea and the birds of the air, over the livestock, over all the earth, and over all the creatures that move along the ground.' So God created man in his own image, in the image of God he created him; male and female he created them (Gen 1:26–27).

Hold on to that. It is the key to everything which follows in human history. It is God's breathtaking organising principle by which we can discover what we are and why we are. The very idea that man—ie, male and female—is made in God's image would have been audacious if it had been dreamed up by Moses or conjured by the apostle Paul. The fact that it is God's explanation of the distinction between ourselves and the rest of creation makes it more readily acceptable. But what does it really mean?

Obviously it means that in some way human beings are like God! In fact, we should note that only human beings, in the whole of creation, were made to be like something, rather Someone, who already existed. Equally obviously that is not a physical likeness. God doesn't have a body. And if it were a physical likeness you would expect people to look more like one another. A glance round any audience or congregation will demonstrate that people are generally dissimilar in appearance!

Before we go rushing on we must hear some theologians question what seems to them a wild goose chase. Luther, for example, understood the image of God to be the 'original righteousness' of Adam and Eve, before they disobeyed God. That was lost at the Fall, when they ate fruit from the forbidden tree. It can only be realised now in Christians. If that is so, bang goes our organising principle since it no longer provides us with something universally true. But it also presents us with a biblical problem. It is inferred later in

Genesis (5:1–2) that the image of God continued in the descendants of Adam and Eve. Some time after they were expelled from Eden we read, 'In the image of God has God made man' (Gen 9:6). We take this, together with other biblical references to the specialness of people, to mean that in some way we still bear the image of God. So on with our search.

For over a thousand years of Christian history the 'image' was thought of as man's rational faculty. It was an outlook which owed more to Greek thought than to the Bible, but nevertheless Christian thinkers as eminent as Augustine taught it. At first sight this is not very promising, until we realise that for most of them, at least before Thomas Aquinas, being rational is not equated with intellectualism.

> The image of God is placed in the rationality of the soul, but the important point is that it is defined (by Augustine) . . . as a capacity to understand and behold God.[2]

That is certainly a characteristic which is peculiar to human beings.

In more recent years theologians have debated the image of God in terms of our capacity to form relationships, particularly with God. Certainly Adam and Eve were able to cope with a close relationship with God in the Garden of Eden. Their closeness to God was disrupted and broken when they sinned and were evicted from the garden, but God arranged for the relationship to be continued, though less intimately. The Old Testament describes the system of worship and approach which God initiated. It is that closer and more personal relationship with God which Jesus restores for those who believe in him. The New Testament tells us that we can 'Come near to God and he will come near to [us]' (Jas 4:8). Which confirms that we have spiritual faculties which can relate to the ultimate spiritual being, God himself.

Another distinguishing facet of the ability to form relationships is that it can take place horizontally, between people and people. That differs from the way animals relate—even though we sometimes see similarities. Human relationships are wonderfully diverse and fascinating.

Will this understanding of the image of God in man fit with our need for a universally relevant principle? Yes, it will. Man's capacity to relate to God is evident in the way he expresses a longing for that relationship. In spite of the apparent agnosticism of Western man we must not ignore the fact that for most people, for most of human history, religion has (and does) form a vital part of life.

It is universally true also on the level of human relationships. Solitariness is not regarded as normal or usual. People live in community. They always have done so. Those communities vary tremendously from one culture to another, but they are a common demonstration that people need people.

Is that it? No, there are other ways in which we are like God. There are characteristics which, again in the created world, are peculiar to people and common to people everywhere. John Calvin, the great Reformer of sixteenth-century Geneva, listed the following 'distinguished endowments' which resulted from God's image in man:

The reason with which they are endowed by which they can distinguish between good and evil; the principle of religion which is planted in them; their (relationships) with each other . . .; the regard to what is becoming, and the sense of shame which guilt awakens in them, as well as their continuing to be governed by laws. All these are clear indications of preeminent celestial wisdom.[3]

More recently a similar view point has been expressed:

Like God, human beings:
(a) exercise dominion or control over the created world (Gen 1:28)
(b) are social beings (Gen 1:26, 2:18) and have a capacity for forming deep personal relationships
(c) have consciences which help us to do what we think is right rather than what is wrong

(d) can think rationally, make decisions and reflect upon what
we have done

(e) appreciate beauty and be creative.[4]

And to these we might add a sense of humour!

The degree to which one or other of the characteristics is
present does not affect the degree to which a person is more,
or less, human. If that were so then we might argue that a
criminal was less of a man than a detective is; an artist might
be more human than a mathematician; a shy girl might be
less human than a brash boy—and so on.

This 'image' concept is something which is universally true.
It includes people of all sorts and sizes, colours and creed,
races and regions. And at the same time it excludes whatever
is not human. The queen bee may rule the hive but her reign
does not extend beyond it. The buzzard may draw a circle
in the air but is no artist.

So there you have our organising principle, our answer to
the question 'What is man?' People are made in the image
of God. This principle in every way satisfies our search for
something which is universally true and relevant. It recognises
all the faults, flaws and failings in people but at the same
time says to them, 'You are wonderful.' God has shown that
being human is not something of which to be ashamed by
becoming a human being himself in the Person of Jesus. That
same Jesus says to us, 'You are worth more than many
sparrows' (Lk 12:7). And if that seems too small a compliment
remember that, because we could not buy our way back to
God, the ultimate price was paid when Jesus died for us—
see 1 Peter 1:18–19 (compare Romans 5:7–8).

The principle in practice

It's time—you may feel long since time—to return to our
main theme. How does all this relate to our concern for
people with mental handicaps? It is absolutely crucial and
fundamental. We might join the current trend and argue that

they have a right to be treated as people, to enjoy what we enjoy, and to be respected. Which is fine while this view is fashionable, but on what basis do we think and act like this? The fashion may change, indeed may already be changing. We need a solid foundation on which to develop a Christian way of thinking about people with mental handicap, a basis which stands on the principle that people are made in the image of God.

It is possible to achieve this because, uniquely, this principle includes them in. It declares that people with mental handicaps are part of the human race alongside of us, not some subsection of humanity which we may include or exclude as we wish. It makes it more difficult to think of them as if they were distinctly, essentially different from ourselves. Rather they are to be included on all counts.

People with mental handicaps can think about, understand and relate to God. Not, perhaps, as theologians, but then, most of us know our limitations at this point. Nor because they have an IQ adequate to the subject. What both the Bible and experience teach us is that these things are 'spiritually discerned' (1 Cor 2:14).

People with mental handicaps can also form relationships. Some are marvellous at friendships. Peter Smith is thoughtful of the needs of others to a degree which humbles his own parents. But it is the son who wears the mental handicap label. Some inveigle their way into other people's hearts even though they cannot speak a word. Lack of speech only closes off one form of communication. Smiles and tears, looks and touches are eloquent in themselves.

The characteristics of God are present in people with mental handicaps in much the same way as in any of us. Rachel's conscience is far more sensitive than mine, so is her capacity for forgiveness. She doesn't paint or write as well as I do. Nor can she argue as I can. But she dances with a grace I admire.

All this being so—and vastly more—on what basis shall we argue that a person of average intelligence has more value than a person with below average intelligence? Will we reduce our humanity and theirs by speaking in terms of economic potential, or lack of it?

The principle of personal value

Having established that people have value we have to consider what this means in practice, with particular reference to people with mental handicaps. The principle of personal value expresses a biblical application of our organising principle.

There are six elements to be identified. Each is vital to the whole, and the whole is incomplete without all of them. It is *a* principle, not a collection of principles.

Individuality

Every person with a mental handicap is a unique individual. Somehow mental handicap triggers a response which makes us want to group some people together as if they were all the same. We don't need to be told that non-handicapped people differ from one another, but we do need to be reminded that this is also true of people with handicaps. No stereotypes, please!

This tendency is particularly accentuated in respect of people with Down's syndrome. This condition does produce several features which result in some similarity of appearance. Generally they look more like their parents than one another. Yet on the basis of superficial similarities generalisations are frequently made that they are all stubborn, like music, are good swimmers, love needlework, are very loving—and more. Such a catalogue of gifts ought actually to give them a high standing in the popularity charts! And for some of them a number of these things are true. But they have as much to do with heredity and environment as with their condition. Tim and Ian are very different people. Mark and Paul are much more alike. So are Rachel and Paula, but not Debbie and Evelyn, or Ruth and Catherine. Each of them is an individual. One likes to dress smartly; another prefers to wear casual clothes. One is good with a needle; the other is all fingers and thumbs. One loves sport; another despises it. In fact it's pretty much what you would expect from people—and it is true across the range and diversity of mental handicaps.

This being so, it is important to see each person with a mental handicap as an individual and to respond accordingly. We must give up speaking of 'the mentally handicapped', and especially using the adjectival phrase 'mentally handicapped' as a noun! Every one of them is as much made in the image of God as the mix of individuals in your church, club, association, factory or office. That in turn will affect how we think and speak and relate to people with mental handicaps.

Integrity

When you are introduced to a total stranger it is usual to assume that he or she is honest, has a degree of self-respect, and has decided to be where he or she is and to meet who he or she is meeting. Similarly, you hope that person will not immediately think of you as a scoundrel, a liar or an incompetent. We will usually assume each other's integrity. That integrity requires that we have a reasonable degree of choice as to what is happening to us, and what has happened to us so far. We decide where we will live and work; how we will spend our leisure; what we will buy with our money.

Such ordinary human experiences may frequently be denied people with mental handicaps. Many have no say as to when they go to bed, what they will wear, where they live, who their friends will be, how they spend their time, whether they will have the light on or off. This is especially true in institutions, large and small, but may also be true in the parental home.

None of us makes all the decisions in our lives because none of us is an island. We don't usually choose our meal from a menu when we are at home! We don't usually decide a family holiday on the say so of one person. We probably discuss redecoration plans with all concerned. That's fine. But imagine how differently you might feel if you were never allowed to express your preferences, especially about those things most personal to you. Or imagine how you might feel if the only choices were non-choices—'Would you like vanilla or neapolitan ice cream?'—when you want custard or ketchup! Frustration would quickly build up because you would feel that you were being denied your personhood. Imagine finding that each morning someone else has decided which dress you will wear or which tie you will put on. Imagine being told to go to bed at 9.30 pm every night. Imagine being sent to live in another home where you knew no one, in a strange place, without so much as the chance to say, 'Yes,' let alone 'No.'

Believe it or not, such are the daily experiences of many people with mental handicaps. Is it because they can't make decisions? By no means. It may be because they make decisions slowly and someone wants to save time. It may be because they don't express themselves plainly so it's simpler not to ask.

What of their integrity? This is something we must recognise in others regardless of their apparent level of ability. People with mental handicaps should be involved in decisions which affect their lives.

Independence

Every teenager's dream of paradise involves being independent! Do you recall how you longed for the day when you could return home at whatever time you chose, with whatever friends you liked, to do whatever suited you, accompanied by music as loud as you could bear? The reality proved somewhat different. We found that we were never able to be fully independent. Our lives were and are linked into other people's lives, whether they are husbands' or wives', parents' or childrens', employers' or employees', or whoever; we are permanently, unavoidably interdependent. Independence is a chimera, a fantasy. Arguably, the desire for independence lay at the root of Adam and Eve's first sin. It suggests arrogance, the priority of my rights over those of other people. If this is what is meant by independence then it cannot have arisen from our organising principle!

Yet independence is something we encourage in our growing children. We recognise the desirability of their 'standing on their own feet'. We try to discourage them from always looking to us to make their decisions. We are no more cruel than the eagle that hustles its fledgling chick out of the nest and over the cliff face. We know they have potential to be realised, development to be experienced. If we hold them too close to us they will be stunted as people and will not come to maturity. Similarly, in a person with a mental handicap all those same needs exist. Such individuals have potential to be realised, growth to take place. Their experience of life must expand so that they become less dependent on others. Only so will they enjoy both independence and interdependence.

Needing support or care is something common to us all. Some need more than others. Among people with mental handicaps some can live very much more independently than others. With a friend or family keeping a watchful eye, ready to give a helping hand with budgeting and legal matters, they may enjoy a reasonable standard of life. Most need more assistance, which tends to result in overprotection from risks and an unduly high level of dependence.

Even for those for whom any significant degree of independence is unrealistic, there is every likelihood that they could be less dependent than they are. For John to feed himself was considered impossible. 'Too handicapped,' it was said by staff in the residential care home—and anyway there wasn't time. It was quicker and simpler for staff to feed him than to fiddle with teaching him and waiting on his slow progress. Then a young woman joined the staff as a care assistant and determined to help John feed himself. It took months of patient encouragement, tolerated rather than helped by other staff. Eventually he could do it, and with what dignity he now approaches mealtimes. That's it, an independence that enriches and fulfils the individual by releasing more of his potential. That is part of the image of God in us finding expression. Build this into your attitude towards people with mental handicaps and you will find yourself looking for possibilities rather than problems, bridges rather than barriers.

Dignity

There is no doubt that things are better now for people with mental handicaps than they were a few decades ago. Life in large institutions was considered preferable for them—and for society. They would live out their meagre existence on wards where there might be one or two toothbrushes for use by several people. Clothes would come from a common store, marked for the laundry by the name of the ward rather than an individual. Indeed they might well be worn without regard to suitability, size or even sex. Nothing reinforced or encouraged a sense of personal dignity. Small wonder that the 'inmates' showed little awareness of their own worth, shuffling slowly from place to place or wandering aimlessly in the extensive grounds.

Although that era is passing a new day has yet to dawn, at least in terms of public attitudes as reflected by the media. In TV, newspaper and radio reports references to mental handicap are usually contrived to be as dramatic as possible. They are, in consequence, rarely positive. One example of this is what could be called the mental age fallacy. You've certainly heard reports like this: 'Mary Smith went missing from near her home in Kendall yesterday. Mary, who is twenty-two years of age, is mentally handicapped with a mental age of a five year old. . . .' Immediately we realise that this is a vulnerable young woman, and we need to be aware of that if we are to feel any concern for her. But we have also received an image of her as childish. Mary is a woman, not a child. She would see herself as a woman, old enough to be married, as her brother was when he was her age. She has twenty-two years experience of life. She is old enough to vote and, in law, to act for herself. It may be that her reading age approximates to that of a five year old, or that her vocabulary is no more than that of a child in infancy, or that her IQ rating is less than 35. But she is not a child.

If you keep company with people who have a mental handicap you will find yourself embarrassed at times at the way other people speak to them. Have you noticed that when adults talk to little children they frequently raise the pitch of their voice and use words and phrases they never use when speaking to other adults? I have heard the same mode of speaking used towards adults with mental handicaps. They are talked down to rather than treated as equals. There are other ways in which the same tendency shows itself—a children's Bible for an adult, a child's picture book, encouraging or tolerating baby-talk, playing with dollies, requiring them to stay in Sunday school classes well below their age level, and so on.

In the early days of A Cause for Concern senior staff were called 'houseparents'. One day a houseparent complained about his title. 'I can't be parent to most of these residents. Some have more experience of life than I have.' The point was taken.

People with mental handicaps must be treated in ways that are appropriate to their age and experience of life. They must be encouraged to dress as adults when they are adults; to talk as adults when they are adults. They frequently have coped with experiences in life, particularly rejection, which many of us would find impossible to bear. They deserve to be treated with respect and dignity. They too are made in the image of God.

Integration

The imaginative work of men like Andrew Reed (see Chapter 4) achieved more than they intended. His dream had been to develop greater independence in mentally handicapped people by training them in specialised and Christian institutions with a view to their returning to live in the community. What happened in the event was that most of them stayed in the institutions. It proved difficult to achieve what Reed had hoped for, and it suited the community to be relieved of this 'problem'. For nearly 150 years, in consequence, the greater part of the population with mental handicaps was segregated in large mental handicap hospitals. This 'separate development' policy was more effective than apartheid has ever been—at least in ensuring separateness.

The organising principle we have recognised confronts us with the fact that people with mental handicaps are people. Their proper and natural place is among people. They should not need to be made part of the community—they are part of the community. As such they should be accepted, even welcomed. This requires that they are integrated into the community.

Integration is a wonderful idea to which most will subscribe, until it means integration where I am—in my street, in my club, in my church, in my youth organisation, in my house group. That is where it needs to happen. They should be where I am—where you are. At first sight this seems a radical notion, but that says more about what our attitudes have been, what our society has chosen in the past, than what is right or good or possible.

This raises particular challenges for church life. The more conservative and traditional the lifestyle of the particular church, the more challenging it is. Integration flows out from our organising principle. Think about it!

Spirituality

No matter how much like the rest of the animal kingdom we may be at times, in this respect we are always distinct from them. We have a soul, a spirit, which lifts us above the animal or mechanical. It is the essence of our humanity. It was breathed into our first parents by God (see Genesis 2:7).

Now it follows that, as the body has needs, so too does the soul. We are made for God and we cannot live satisfyingly without him. Sooner or later that need catches up with us and overtakes us. We need a relationship with God as much as the body needs food and drink, as much as fire needs oxygen. That's the way we are made. It's not an optional extra, or an appendage we can decide to cut off.

To the extent that this is true, it is true for everyone. People with mental handicaps are not different in this respect. That means that they must hear the good news that God loves them and has shown his love in Jesus. They must hear in a way they can understand and to which they can respond. Those who do respond must have opportunity to become part of the church, the body of Christ. They must be nurtured and helped to grow as Christians. They must be encouraged in their own service of God.

All of it is possible, even for people with very severe handicaps. Their greatest handicap is not so much their condition but our attitudes, we who are the church. So we must adjust more than they. We must consider what the obstacles are to the people with mental handicaps who form part of our own congregation or who live in our own parish or district. We must give thought to how we will remove those obstacles and make a way for those people to be reached and nurtured in Christ. We must consider how they will take a meaningful place within the church and how they will have opportunity to grow by serving. Think about it!

If you are still with me, we have travelled a long way together in this chapter. We have crossed a desert and, hopefully, there is no going back. Any trace of the attitudes which exclude, discriminate against, or dehumanise people with mental handicaps will be inexcusable in us. And now you can begin to recognise and relate to people whom you will come to appreciate and value increasingly. If we can succeed in this we will be among the few in the history of the church who have achieved this. That being so, who can tell what blessings will be given to us, as the Bible says, 'pressed down and running over'!

Notes

[1] D. Cairns, *The Image of God in Man* (SCM Press: London, 1953), p 69.

[2] *Ibid*, p 96.

[3] J. Calvin, *Commentary on Psalm 8*, quoted by D. Cairns, *ibid*.

[4] M. Eden, D. Potter, T. Thompson, *No Handicaps Please, We're Christians* (Causeway: UK, 1990), p 6.

3
What's the Difference?

We had to recognise how much alike we are before we could assess differences between us. It doesn't bother us to discover that our friend has brown eyes whereas our own are blue. We don't fret that the friend might be non-normal because we already know that personhood is not decided on eye colour. Similarly, now that we know what we mean by 'people' we can look at differences between them without wondering whether they really are people or not.

We are now ready to take a closer look at what the differences appear to be in respect of mental handicap. We need something akin to measurements and descriptions to set alongside of each other for comparisons to be possible. We should be able to find out for what reasons and in what ways the differences exist. And we need to look at statistics to gain some idea of the scale of the issues which concern us. As we do so it will become increasingly clear that mental handicap is not to be confused with mental illness. They are distinct and different conditions.

Definitions

Let's start with definitions. We are well on in our considera-tion of mental handicap but we have yet to say what it is! Once we know who or what we are talking about we can consider causes and consequences. We will be able also to think about statistics. If that sounds reasonably straight-forward, don't be deceived. Very little is straightforward in respect of mental handicap!

Our first difficulty when we come to attempt definitions of mental handicap is the sheer diversity of people we want to define. There are hundreds of thousands of them, and you know from experience that it is difficult to describe, let alone define, any group of people. Try it. Think about your church and the people you saw there last Sunday. Now try to define them. Difficult, isn't it, especially if you try to be fairly brief? You might define them in terms of their common interest in religion—perhaps they are all Christians. You might define them in terms of class—perhaps they are all middle class! But there are so many ways in which your definition will fall short—in terms of social life, education, age, medical history, and so on. Given enough time and paper you might manage to describe them, but not define them. If you don't go to church, try defining the people you meet in the Conservative club, or the union meeting, or at the football ground. You might manage a definition of their common interest, but you will be hard pressed to define them. (No wonder we have problems when we try to find a neat label we can pin on this condition.)

Strangely, however, we are expected to define mental handicap without difficulty. Yet the thousands of people in Britain who have a mental handicap come from every social class, most age groups and live in every town. In ability they are immensely varied. In tastes and interests they differ widely. In appearance they are often indistinguishable from others in a crowd.

So the attempt at definition will be approached with some caution. We are not likely, in one or two sentences, to define adequately the variety of people with mental handicaps whom we may know or meet. The best we can hope for is that we identify more clearly different aspects of mental handicap.

There are four main approaches to definition, which tend to be functional rather than personal—that is, they define what the person does (or otherwise) rather than what the person is. These are medicine, education, law and sociology.

Medical definitions

The medical profession is in the front line when it comes to identifying mental handicap in babies and infants. The role of the pediatrician is often crucial in recognising that a child has a condition which causes or contributes to mental handicap. Already we have acknowledged the difficulty faced by those who perform this role—and we have also to admit that the results are, at times, negative.

> One version of differences—the medical version—has had a dominating influence, far outstripping that warranted by the physical conditions that many mentally handicapped people do suffer from. Mental handicap provides a case study of the 'medicalisation' of a social problem. . . . Medicine—its institutions, personnel, concept, and modes of explaining behaviour—has been the main instrument for excluding mentally handicapped people from society.[1]

That exclusion has diminished in recent years with the programme of closing hospitals for mentally handicapped people. The conditions which they have endured in such institutions for the last 100 years is no compliment to the medical practitioners.

> The medical profession has knowingly administered a most deplorable standard of life to the mentally handicapped people in its care. The lack of protest from within the medical profession about this has undoubtedly been aided by the fact that they are seen, in strict medical terms, as incurable and therefore hopeless.[2]

Identifying people according to their defined differentness tends to exclude them from the ranks of those who are called 'normal'. Medical definitions inevitably suffer this tendency. Although the causes of mental handicap are largely unknown, those conditions which can be described and defined are explained in language and terms which are almost incomprehensible to the untrained person.

A widely used, but wholly negative definition of mental handicap comes from the American Psychiatric Association:

(a) Significantly sub-average intellectual functioning, an IQ test of 70 or below in an individually administered IQ test.
(b) Concurrent deficits or impairments in adaptive behaviour taking the person's age into consideration.
(c) Onset of the intellectual impairment before the age of eighteen years.[3]

The medical profession has, without question, made significant contributions in the field of mental handicap but, as is already apparent, we need to note that we are not considering a disease or an illness. It is a fact that people with mental handicaps often have physical as well as intellectual difficulties —spasticity, epilepsy, heart defects—and that their life expectancy may, as a result, be lower than the national average. But they are not ill.

Educational definitions

Education brings the issue close to us and, currently, probably has a greater influence on the lives of people with mental handicaps and their place in society than the medical profession. Here definitions are almost always in terms of intelligence or lack of it, usually expressed as IQ test results. These tests are now a widespread means of assessing a person's level of intelligence. The limitations are widely acknowledged, but they continue to dominate definitions and descriptions of mental handicap and the people affected.

Necessary to the IQ test are assumptions about what is normal, but those assumptions are not necessarily accurate. For example:

Growth in intelligence is not steady for everyone, and is particularly variable in the growth spurts in individuals in puberty. . . . In adolescence the stresses of school or work throw up more candidates for the label 'mentally handicapped'.[4]

Until 1971 severely handicapped children were excluded from education and received 'training' from health authority units. From 1981 the notion of handicap was dropped from the Education Act of that year in favour of a requirement to identify any child with special needs. This definition 'embraces children with significant learning difficulties and emotional or behavioral disorders as well as those with disabilities of body or mind'.[5]

IQ tests bring education and medicine together in the form of the World Health Organisation definition of degrees of mental handicap:

Category of mental handicap	IQ measurement of intelligence
Profound	below 20
Severe	20–35
Moderate	36–51
Mild	52–70 or 75

Perhaps it is the use of IQ scores that feeds the unhelpful notion of mental age, commonly beloved by the media. It assumes that a person with an IQ of, say, 50, will have a mental age of half his actual age. That this is an inaccurate way of viewing the person is self-evident, but none the less it persists.

Legal definitions

The third major category of definition is the law. Any attempt to safeguard the interests or concerns of a particular group in society requires that such a group is clearly identifiable. The Mental Health Act 1983, as well as distinguishing between mental handicap and mental illness, defines two categories which relate to mental handicap:

> —'severe mental impairment'—a state of arrested or incomplete development of mind which includes severe impairment of intelligence and social functioning and is associated with abnormally aggressive or seriously irresponsible conduct on the part of the person concerned;
> —'mental impairment'—a state of arrested or incomplete development of mind (not amounting to severe mental impairment) which includes significant impairment of intelligence and social functioning and is associated with abnormally aggressive or seriously irresponsible conduct on the part of the person concerned.[6]

The legal position is complex because of the extent to which it focuses on a person's capacity or incapacity. Both of the legal definitions make a link between disability and crime by referring to aggressive behaviour. This then enables a lawyer to claim diminished responsibility on the part of the person with the mental handicap—but this in turn unhelpfully implies that aggression or seriously irresponsible behaviour is to be expected from a person with a mental handicap.

Incapacity has been at the heart of debates following cases in 1987 and 1989 in respect of imposed sterilisation of women with mental handicaps. Even here it is not a simple matter of whether the person is capable of making a decision or not. In respect of medical treatment, the person must understand what is being proposed and the consequences of such action. In respect of contracts, the person must be 'capable of understanding the general nature' of what he is doing. In respect of making a will that would be inadequate. In this case the mentally handicapped person must be able to understand what he is doing *and* he must be able to remember what property he has to dispose of in his will *and* he must be aware of his obligations to relatives and others.

Sociological definitions

By sociological definition I mean that which relates to social services departments. We have neither space nor need to plunge into the murky waters of scientific sociology! Professor Joan Bicknell quotes a student's definition of mental handicap as 'a person who, through developmental intellectual handicap requires special services to lead an ordinary life'.[7]

From this perspective, focus is on the services required by particular groups of people living in the community. Once medicine or education have designated a person as having a mental handicap, it becomes a matter of concern for the social services. They may allocate a social worker to provide the family with support and to explain access to services the local authority provides for the person. In 1993 social services departments became responsible for ensuring that services and facilities are available, as necessary, to assist people with mental handicaps to live in the community. For future planning of their resources they need to know who the mentally handicapped people are in their area and what their needs are likely to be.

You may well feel that all this has not helped a great deal. Hopefully you have a clearer idea why the issue is unclear! Definitions are not easy to arrive at and even harder to apply.

It will be clear that:

theories emphasise how mentally handicapped people are different and inferior compared to others; there is much less emphasis on how they are similar.[8]

More significantly:

these definitions tell us very little about what individual people can actually do or what their personality will be. It is important to remember that, whatever the degree of mental handicap, learning is still possible.[9]

With so much unresolved, it may assist if we at least define some of the commonly used terms.

1 Impairment. This refers to some difference resulting from physical or brain-related factors. It leads to some 'loss of function' intellectually or physically, or both.

2 Disability. The impairment disables the person so that he or she is restricted in some way. This generally relates to things most people are able to do or achieve—walking, talking, looking after one's self, and so on. It will also affect ability to perform more complex tasks and may affect ability to grasp ideas and concepts.

3 Handicap. The society in which the disabled person lives is organised in such a way that his 'difference' becomes a handicap. For example, a person may be disabled by arthritis, but is handicapped by having to climb steps into the post office; a person may be disabled by brain damage, but is handicapped by having to read and complete a form before he can claim benefits.

Mental handicap might be described as mental disability. It becomes a handicap because of the demands of our educated, high tech, fast moving civilisation. Proper organisation and support would reduce the handicapping effects of society for such people.

Causes

If definitions are hard to come by, we might hope for some certainty when it comes to causes. Hope on!

There is a story about a medical student who was taking his final oral examination and was answering all the questions very well indeed; he knew he was doing well. The professor was impressed and was almost finished. Then he said, 'Just one final question, Mr Johnson. What is the cause of Down's syndrome?' The question worried the student because he did not want to end the examination in an unsatisfactory way. He hesitated and then answered, 'I'm sorry, professor, I did know but I have forgotten.'

The professor looked at the student sadly and said, 'That's a great pity, Mr Johnson, because now nobody knows.'[10]

This probably fictional story pretty well sums up our difficulty. You could say that we face two problems—ignorance and ignorance! We share the ignorance of professionals because most of the causes of mental handicap have not been identified.

In one survey of [mentally handicapped] hospital patients Leck [1967] found no identifiable cause for subnormality in over 70% of cases.[11]

A professor of genetics made the same point more elegantly:

Genetic factors are of major importance in almost all forms of mental retardation, but it is only in a minority of cases that one can identify a specific disorder with a recognisable genetic basis.[12]

And this, in spite of a century of sustained medical investigation.

The second type of ignorance is that which comes from not understanding medical terminology and jargon. 'Chromosomal abnormalities' and 'metabolic disorders' are relatively simple terms compared with descriptions of complex or obscure medical conditions. Try this description of homocystinuria:

Autosomal Recessive. Most of those affected have reduced or absent cystathionine synthethase, an enzyme in the pathway converting methionine to cystine. . . .[13]

If we are careful to keep our objective in mind—to be in a better position to understand and respond to people with mental handicaps—we can manage with a relatively simple approach to the causes of mental handicap. Professionals will find this deficient, even irritating. However, hopefully they will forgive the inadequacy of this approach as they approve the goal.

We can divide the causes broadly into two groups—first, those which are physical; second, those which are social and environmental. There is overlap and interaction between the two which is beyond the scope of our concern to examine.

Physical causes

Almost all forms of profound, severe or moderate mental handicap are the result of some damage to or difference in the central nervous system—the brain. This may be due to differences in chromosomal or genetic make-up. Chromosomes and genes are part of the body's blueprint, found in every cell and determining most of our human characteristics from hair colour to personality. By far the most common form of mental handicap characterised by different chromosome structure is Down's syndrome. It is the consequence of an extra chromosome in each cell from the moment of conception. 'The primary cause of Down's syndrome is one of the unsolved mysteries of human genetics.'[14]

Differences of genetic make-up also result in what are called 'neural tube defects', which affect 1 in every 500 live births. The best known of these is spina bifida, and between 40 per cent and 50 per cent of spina bifida children are intellectually impaired.

Chromosomal anomalies never increase potential. 'All such anomalies reduce mental and physical ability, usually to a profound degree.'[15] The baby in the womb is vulnerable to infection and any breakdown in the processes by which it is nourished. The absence of certain enzymes may cause brain damage, though the effects may, in some instances, be minimised by dietary measures after birth—as in phenylketonuria.

The physical dependence of the unborn baby on the mother may also result in mental handicap. It will be adversely affected if the mother suffers from certain diseases during pregnancy such as rubella (German measles), chicken-pox, and now AIDS. Drugs taken during pregnancy may impair brain function in the baby, including alcohol and nicotine.

Complications at the time of birth may cause mental handicap in the young child which might have been a normal fetus. The complication occurs during the actual process of birth, caused by difficulties in labour, or oxygen starvation. A delay in breathing after birth can damage brain cells, causing cerebral palsy and brain damage.[16]

To repeat: profound, severe and moderate mental handicap are the result of some damage to or difference of the central nervous system. It occurs in children in all social classes and it is scattered throughout the general population. The extent to which a child develops while having one of these conditions will be affected significantly by the extent to which the person is accepted and assisted. Where a community loves and supports individuals with a mental handicap, their prospects are substantially better than where they suffer rejection by or estrangement from the community or their family. There is a social dimension to mental handicap!

Social and environmental causes

It is reasonably obvious that a child growing up undernourished, with little or no formal education, having to work on the family plot of ground, is likely to be at a disadvantage when compared with a child who is well fed, attending school and spending his leisure time playing with friends and parents. It is therefore not altogether surprising to learn that a proportion of all cases of mental handicap—including mild cases—are not caused by genetic anomalies or medical problems as such. The environment of the child's upbringing— including poverty, lack of stimulus, insufficient educational standards, weak family structures—will have negative effects. Some research suggests that as many as two-thirds of children are within the range 50 to 75 IQ for these reasons. More controversially, a link is sometimes made between social causes of mental handicap and social class, with the sugges- tion that a high proportion of people with mild mental handicaps have parents who are unskilled workers.

We ought not to hide our ignorance of the causes of mental handicap by some pseudo-scientific ploy that effectively blames parental or social factors which may or may not lie at the root of the issue. While we explain one child's mental handicap in terms of his deprived environment, we may take no account of the fact that his brother has not been adversely affected by the same circumstances!

Yet, at the same time, society must bear due responsibility for the handicapping effects suffered by children in poor areas. It is usually in such districts that schools are overcrowded, are likely to be understaffed, have high numbers of children who use English as a second language or come from disturbed family backgrounds. It is the children of such schools who should be attracting the commitment of the state and the community to ensure that the enormous difficulties they face do not result in long-term intellectual inadequacy. And dare we contemplate the possible effects of famine and poverty on the children of Third-World countries for generations to come as 20 per cent of the world's population consumes 80 per cent of the world's resources?

Sobering, isn't it! Even if this were true only for a handful of people it would challenge our lifestyles. It is time to ask just how many people are affected by mental handicaps.

Statistics

Mental handicap causes statisticians headaches, and their computers, burn-out. To say the figures available are imprecise is almost to exaggerate their accuracy. In the first place mental handicap doesn't have to be registered by anyone with anyone. Local authorities are increasingly setting up registers of the people with mental handicaps in their area who use the services they and the health authority provide for them. These probably include a large proportion, but they are by no means regarded as comprehensive. Which goes some way towards explaining why government official figures tend to be rather low and those of charities and campaigners tend to be much higher.

In research for this book I have looked at figures till I am cross-eyed. For me, too much information results in less understanding rather than more. So I will keep this simple!

Professional sources estimate that profound, severe and moderate mental handicap occurs at a rate of about 3 or 4 per 1,000 of the population. Mild mental handicap is ten times more common. This would give us a figure of not less than 33 people per 1,000 as having a mental handicap. The population of the United Kingdom was 57 million in 1988, which would give us a figure of 1,880,000 people with mental handicaps. Most sources find that difficult to admit so usually settle for a lower figure of around 1,250,000—or 1 in every 45 people.

What *is* the difference?

You will already anticipate that there is no simple answer to the question. You may think that this book is too political— ie, incapable of giving straight answers to straight questions! In fact the problem is with the subject matter rather than the writer.

There is as much difference between people with mental handicaps as there is in the population at large. What we will attempt here is to identify the three best known types of mental handicap and to describe some of the features of those particular conditions. Please remember that every person who has one of these conditions is an individual with a distinct personality of his own.

Down's syndrome

This is the most readily recognised form of mental handicap and also the most common among those with severe or moderate mental handicap. It accounts for about one-third of all people with severe mental handicaps.

There are some individuals whose intelligence is within the normal range and quite a number who could be described as only mildly handicapped. Yet they have in common a slightly oriental appearance which gave rise to the first descriptive label, mongol. Anyone who knows children with Down's syndrome well will agree that they resemble their parents more than they resemble each other.[17]

This condition has been known from ancient times. There is evidence that people with Down's syndrome were revered by the Olmecs of ancient Mexico. It was not, however, a subject for serious study until the 1860s when Dr J. Langdon Down published a manual for the identification and training of people with this condition. The term 'mongolian' was used, not only because of the oriental appearance of those affected, but also because it was thought to be a degeneration to a more primitive stage in human development. At the time Darwinism was very popular and some explanation for the failure of evolution had to be given.

The genetic impact of Down's syndrome results in an extra chromosome in every cell of the person's body. This is true in most cases—there is a related condition affecting some cells only. However, the cause of Down's syndrome is not known. A link can be drawn between the age of the mother and the incidence of Down's syndrome: at 20 years of age it occurs in 1 in 2,000 births; at 35 years of age it occurs in 1 in 750 births; at 45 years of age it occurs in 1 in 300 births, reducing to 1 in 60 above that age. While an older mother is more likely to give birth to a baby with Down's syndrome, the majority of mothers are between twenty and twenty-nine years of age simply because this is the period when women are most likely to become mothers!

As well as affecting intellectual development in varying degrees, Down's syndrome has several physical characteristics which make people with this condition easily recognisable. These include small slanted eyes, a short flat nose and a short neck; additionally, some have heart defects and most are susceptible to infection.

It is not so long ago that children with Down's syndrome would rarely live into adulthood. In 1929 the mean survival age was only nine years. A survey in the 1980s showed that the mean survival age is now over forty years. This is the result of better medical care being available and may also reflect well on the participation of people with Down's syndrome in sports and games.

It is common to hear parents and those who work with people with Down's syndrome speak with great affection for them. Yet the future of babies with Down's syndrome is in greater jeopardy than ever before. It is one of the few handicapping conditions which can be diagnosed before birth and, a widely held view within the medical profession is that such babies should be aborted. In 1990 the law was changed to make this possible, right up to the moment of birth.

Autism

Autism and Down's syndrome have in common the fact that the causes of both conditions are almost unknown in spite of extensive research over very many years. Beyond that they share few similarities. Although less common, autism is thought to affect 4 or 5 in every 10,000 of the population.

The film *Rain Man* did a good deal to bring autism to public attention. Although the main character was portrayed as having a remarkable island of ability, typical of an uncommon form of autism, he also demonstrated vividly the obsessions and aloofness common to the condition.

Autism was first described as recently as 1943 by Dr Leo Kanner. He identified three primary features:
1 A profound failure to develop social relationships and an aloneness he termed 'autism'.
2 An obsessional desire for sameness represented by a dislike of change in routine and environment.
3 An onset within the first two years of life.

Autism is associated with severe mental handicap in about

half of those affected, with about a quarter in the mild mental handicap category.

There are no obvious physical characteristics associated with autism. People with autism tend to maintain 'social distance', generally avoiding physical or eye contact with other people. Speech and other forms of communication are likely to be limited, with a tendency to echo words or phrases.

Autistic children often insist obsessionally on a particular routine in their daily lives, and their resistance to change—either of routine or of objects or people in their environment—creates major management problems. Some children develop a deep attachment to an unusual object, such as a piece of string or a cup, from which they cannot easily be parted. These behaviours have been interpreted as an attempt by the child to create some order and constancy in a confusing and chaotic world.[18]

When distressed, autistic people are likely to pull faces, jump, walk on toes, flap hands or become engrossed with their fingers. Rages and tantrums may result in aggression to themselves or others with no apparent cause.

Cerebral palsy

Cerebral palsy is defined as a group of disorders characterised by abnormal movement and muscle tone due to defects of or damage to the brain during early life. The condition is not progressive, but it invariably alters in character as the child becomes older.[19]

This condition is usually associated with physical disability rather than mental handicap. Indeed it is not uncommon to come across people with cerebral palsy who are of average or above average intelligence. However, some forms of cerebral palsy do result in significant mental handicap.

For about 20 per cent of people affected no cause can be identified. In about 75 per cent the cause is likely to have occurred shortly before birth, during birth, or in the first week following birth. Toxaemia late in pregnancy, difficulties in labour, resuscitation at birth and acute problems immediately after birth may lead to cerebral palsy. There are various forms of the condition, classified according to the way in which it affects movements or lack of it. Those which are more severe are likely to be associated with mental handicap.

What we have been trying to do is to identify what the differences are between people with mental handicaps and those who are not handicapped. We have seen that there are physical, intellectual and social factors resulting in differences. Which suggests that there are likely to be variations affecting every aspect of life and experience.

But how much do those differences and variations matter? Of course it matters if they reveal some obvious, preventable cause of mental handicap, but we have seen that that is unlikely. The medical profession is befuddled and embarrassed by the fact that much of its vast body of knowledge is based on speculation and guesswork! The reason these differences matter is that they may fall outside of what we are comfortable with, what we accept as normal.

As we have noted, we tend to call 'normal' what is only average. We use various criteria to decide the range, including education, culture and morality. But these are themselves variable from one country to another, from one era to another. In Britain a son brings pride to his father's heart if he gets a degree; whereas a South American Indian may glow with pride when his son shoots a wild pig with a bow and arrow.

Being human is normal, and that takes into account much greater diversity than our usual criteria will allow. So some people are side-lined—for example, criminals are sometimes described as 'animals', people in remote tribes may be described as 'barbaric'. And people with mental handicaps may be treated as if they are non-persons. We need to recognise that it is our categories of 'normalness' that are too

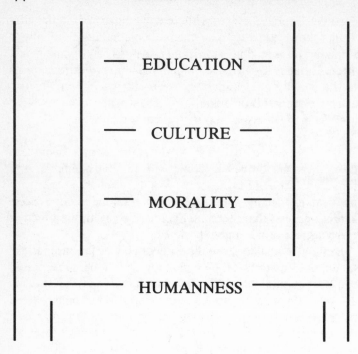

Figure 1

narrow, resulting in a limited and blinkered outlook (see Figure 1).

We are making progress together. We know that people are people regardless of differences between them. We have discovered, perhaps to our surprise, that people with mental handicaps have far more in common with non-handicapped people than differences from them. We can recognise some of the ways in which we differ from one another and, hopefully, are better able to accept each other. In fact, viewed from the theological perspective we outlined earlier, many of the difficult issues disappear and others seem much more manageable. This being so, one would expect to see it reflected in the life and activity of Christians and the church down through the centuries. Not so, at least not to the extent one would anticipate.

Notes

[1] J. Ryan, *The Politics of Mental Handicap* (Free Association Books: London, 1987), p 15.

[2] *Ibid*.

[3] M. Craft, J. Bicknell, S. Hollins (eds), *Mental Handicap* (Balliere Tindall: London, 1985), p 78.

[4] *Ibid*, p 79.

[5] S. Hollins and M. Grimer, *Going Somewhere* (SPCK: London, 1988), p 8.

[6] Quoted in *Mentally Incapacitated Adults and Decision Making* (HMSO: London, 1991), p 23.

[7] J. Bicknell, in *Mental Handicap op cit*, p 5.

[8] Ryan, *op cit*, p 27.

[9] Hollins, *op cit*, p 9.

[10] B. Stratford, *Down's Syndrome: Past, Present and Future* (Penguin: London, 1989), p 1.

[11] I. Macdonald, in *Special Education: Policy, Practice and Social Issues* (Harper & Row: London, 1981), p 90.

[12] P. Harper, in *Mental Handicap, op cit*, p 89.

[13] *Ibid* p 100.

[14] Stratford, *op cit*.

[15] M. Craft, *Mental Handicap, op cit* p 84.

[16] R. Senior, *Towards a Better Understanding* (Euromonitor: London, 1985), p 20.

[17] Stratford, *op cit*.

[18] I. Kolvin, in *Mental Handicap, op cit*, p 150.

[19] G. Hosking, *ibid*, p 128.

4
What's Happened?

'The present state of things is the consequence of the former.'
So said the sensible Dr Johnson. The way things are today
is a result of the way they were yesterday. Different, maybe.
Better, we hope. But 'now' has grown out of 'then' and,
inevitably, 'then' has influenced the shape of 'now'. That is
why history is significant.

Mental handicap is nothing new. If, with all the advantages
of modern medical science, babies with mental handicaps are
born today then they must also have been born to previous
generations of parents. For example, the numbers of babies
with Down's syndrome are born as a more or less uniform
proportion of live births around the world, regardless of
wealth, poverty or social status. It is probable that a similar
proportion of babies with Down's syndrome have been born
throughout history. If, today, some forms of mental handicap
are due to poor environment, inadequate stimulus, mal-
nourishment, then the likelihood exists that in times when
these problems were more widespread than now they would
have had similar consequences. Mental handicap is certainly
not a new phenomenon.

It may, therefore, seem strange that mental handicap does
not have much of a history. Those who have tried to unearth
the facts have found the evidence fragmentary and contra-
dictory. As we have already seen, the Olmecs of ancient
Mexico appear to have regarded people with Down's syndrome

76

as, at the very least, objects of interest. The statues and figurines discovered by archaeologists suggest they may even have thought of them as divine visitors. The Athenians, by contrast:

> exposed handicapped children on the hillsides, either to die of starvation or to be devoured by wild animals. This deliberate neglect and abandonment was countenanced by the Laws of Lycurgus and was practised mainly from motives of concern that developmental handicap should not be passed on, but also there seems to have been a fear of 'madmen' or those who might do things contrary to good Greek custom.[1]

> Historical accounts of mental handicap tend to be mainly concerned with institutional and legal landmarks—the building of an asylum, the passing of Acts of Parliament. Or they deal with the acts of great men—scientific discoveries and educational reforms. . . . Virtually nothing is known of the lives of idiots and their families. Mentally handicapped people are still as hidden from history as they are from the rest of life. What history they do have is not so much theirs as the history of others acting either on their behalf, or against them.[2]

In Britain one of the earliest distinct references to mental handicap was in legislation passed in 1325! Edward II's Act of Parliament, *De Praerogative Regis*, protected their property rights. It also drew a distinction between mental illness and mental handicap. Regrettably that distinction was then more or less forgotten until the end of the nineteenth century. Which is another reason for the relative absence of a history of mental handicap. People with mental illness (usually referred to as lunatics) and people with mental handicaps (usually referred to as idiots) were regarded as the same or so similar as not to warrant separate mention or treatment.

When we turn to discover what Christians have said or done in response to mental handicap it is almost impossible to find a history. No book or substantial article on the subject seems ever to have been written! Professional interest in mental handicap flourished in Europe around 1800. From then on a religious response to the issues can be traced, but a near silence hangs over the preceding centuries. Furthermore, the bias and priorities of historians have largely ignored the religious motivation of many reformers in the field.

Christians who live by the example of Jesus will bring benefits to their community regardless of the laws of the land or the normal function of contemporary culture. Their day-to-day lives touch those of other people, especially those in need, so as to bring relief and benefit. Such ordinary expressions of the love of God do not necessarily result in major movements or institutions. The evidence of history and the Bible is that this has been the case. This 'informal' caring made life better and brighter for slaves, prisoners, outcasts and poor people. It would be reasonable to assume that people with mental handicaps were also beneficiaries.

One further comment must be made before we pitch into the subject. We must remember that those whose work we review were men and women of their day. We will be tempted to judge their work by our own standards, forgetting that the social climate in which they lived and toiled was different from our own. If now we see further than they did it is because we stand on their shoulders!

One of the first references to mental handicap found in Christian history is in a sermon by Clement of Alexandria (AD 150–220). He was critical of the practice of using people with mental handicaps as clowns, for the entertainment of the rich, on the basis that it was inconsistent with the purity of life required by God's word.

By the middle of the fourth century, following the conversion of Constantine, Christian institutions for the poor, the sick, and for children were being encouraged by church councils. Daniel Defoe made the brief comment about this early period that:

> Idiots were denied the communion in the primitive churches, but I never read that they were not to be prayed for or were not admitted to hear.[3]

It is unfortunate that he does not name his source.

An attractive legend links St Nicholas with mentally handicapped people. He is best known as the original Father Christmas and patron saint of children, wayfarers and scholars. Through his recognition of and care for 'imbeciles' and 'idiots' he is said to be the protector of the 'feeble-minded' as well. He was supposedly Bishop of Myra at a time when Diocletian was persecuting the churches. Sadly, however, the saint was probably legendary!

Euphrasia, a sister of Emperor Theodosius who died in AD 394, entered a convent in Egypt to care for people with mental handicaps. Basil 'the Great', another bishop of the fourth century, built a large Christian complex outside Caeserea. It included hospitals and hostels for the poor and sick, and a special unit for the insane for whom he had definite sympathies.

Augustine of Hippo (AD 354–430)—the St Augustine of *The Confessions*—makes reference to mentally handicapped people (whom he calls *moriones*) in the course of refuting heresy. 'Who could bear to see the image of God . . . born feebleminded . . .?' This would seem to deny humanness to people with mental handicaps. However, the drift of his argument is that each person inherits the influence of original sin from his parents. This mars the image of God in every human being. If this were not so we would have to explain how an unblemished image of God could exist in people more obviously imperfect than others may appear. Augustine's intention was to refute the already common argument that illness and handicap was a direct result of parental sin. He wished to include people with mental handicaps with the rest of humanity as full members of the race. His writings pay touching tribute to a Christian known to him who had a mental handicap.

During the Middle Ages (500–1500) it is generally assumed that people with mental handicaps were accepted in their small-scale rural communities. During this period 'insanity was considered part of everyday life, and fools and madmen walked the streets.'[4] Even so, it is also probable that they were treated as objects of derision and the butt of cruelty. 'Peasants ragged the village idiot no less than sightseers jostled the Bedlamites.'[5]

In this period it was the church that preserved all that remained of classical medicine. Monasteries then provided the closest thing to hospital care. Undoubtedly people with mental infirmities were included with the poor and destitute for whom they cared. In 491 monks in Jerusalem established an asylum for the insane. Another was established in Cologne in 560. The Archbishop of Metz built a monastery for the mentally infirm in 850. A skull of a girl who had Down's syndrome has been found near the site of a Saxon monastery in Leicestershire, suggesting that she and others may have been cared for there. Not that monastic life was always a pleasant experience! Franciscans specialised in daily whippings. Some clerics specialised in exorcisms. Among the therapeutic aids listed in one establishment were manacles, iron chains, padlocks and stocks!

People with mental disorders were also helped in a few of the medieval hospitals. These were infirmaries run by monks, relieving a wide variety of needy persons as well as providing hospitality for pilgrims. Of the 750 known to have flourished, the earliest example on record in Britain is that at York, referred to by King Athelstan in 937. There was a hospital at Chester for 'poor silly people' before the time of Henry III (1216–1272). By the twelfth century St Bartholomew's, Smithfield, received people with mental disabilities together with those who were deaf, dumb, blind and crippled; including one with an 'akynge hede' and another with 'ryngyng of his erys'. St Mary Magdelene's was on a pilgrim route at Holloway near Bath. Known as Holy Cross Hospital, it too received people with mental handicaps.

The best known medieval hospital was Bethlem, London, adapted specifically for the care of lunatics in 1377, having begun as a priory of the Order of the Star of Bethlehem. It became a notorious institution and was the subject of inquiries from time to time. Although not included in its original charter, it is known to have received people with mental handicaps.

A common form of mental handicap in the Middle Ages was cretinism, a condition caused by a thyroid deficiency and thought to be linked to defective drinking water. In the Pyrenees cretins were regarded with some awe, and it is thought that 'cretin' is a derivation of 'Christian', which may allude to their being regarded as too simple to sin. It was not until the sixteenth century that the condition was to be described scientifically and linked with mental handicap—and this was to be achieved by two Protestant ministers.

The church's care of people with mental handicaps during this period reflected the superstitions which were characteristic of the community at large. It was generally assumed that the causes were probably demonic. Peter Abelard broke with convention by teaching that mental disorders have natural causes—which drew protest from Bernard of Clairvaux.

Renaissance and reformation (AD 1400–1600)

This was an era distinguished by the blossoming of learning and the rediscovery of biblical truth. Feudalism was coming to an end, and with it the breaking down of tightly knit rural communities. Disadvantaged groups began to gravitate to the towns, bringing people with mental handicaps together with beggars, paupers, people with physical disabilities, and criminals. Social unrest gave rise to the Poor Laws and the beginnings of the workhouse. Some of the inmates were inevitably people with mental handicap. The dissolution of the monasteries removed their previous places of refuge.

The state began to take more control of caring facilities. Bethlem was given by Henry VIII to the City of London in 1547. With the rise of civil power in this field the activity of the church declined. As a result it becomes more difficult to speak of the church's response to people with mental handicaps. Attention focuses rather on the activities of individual believers.

Attitudes, however, did not change significantly. The view persisted that mental disorders were caused by the devil or his agents. Among those who were executed, by Catholics and Protestants, for being witches were women who were mentally handicapped. Samuel Harsnett, Archbishop of York, relatively enlightened and dismissive of witchcraft, lists as five classes of culprits 'children, fools, women, cowards, sick or black melancholic discomposed wits'. 'The most senseless and ignorant creatures that could be found' and 'witless persons with scarcely a clue as to what happened to them' were accused in the 1692 Salem witch trials in New England.

It's time we went back a few years to Martin Luther. He has a very 'bad press' in the field of mental handicap. The textbooks which mention him do so derogatively, and the slander is even repeated in Sunday papers and magazines. He is accused of teaching that people with mental handicaps have no soul and should be drowned. Which is a serious allegation!

Luther is reputed to have told his friends the story of a tussle he had with a twelve-year-old boy in Dessau. The boy was apparently mentally handicapped and behaved in a disgusting manner. Luther is said to have advised the Prince of Anhalt: 'If I were the Prince, I should take this child to the Moldau River which flows near Dessau and drown him.' The advice was refused. He then suggested: 'Well then the Christians shall order the Lord's Prayer to be said in church and pray that the dear Lord take the Devil away.' This was done daily in Dessau and the 'changeling' died in the following year.[6]

The incident bears closer examination in two respects. First, we need to understand the way mental handicap was commonly understood in his day. A child with a deformity or mental handicap was said to be not the baby as it was born to its mother, but a replacement left by fairies or demons. This view was adapted from pagan folklore and Christianised. Explanations for this strange exchange were that the parents were guilty of some wickedness, or that the parents loved the child more than they loved God, or that the mother had been seduced by the devil. If Luther should reflect in some respects the religious culture of his day we should not be surprised.

Second, we need to enquire whether the source of the story is reliable. It is found in Luther's *Table Talk*. This is a collection of conversations between Luther and friends at dinner. It was written and edited by various people and is not regarded as reliable by scholars of Luther. The remarks were not written up at the time and may have included stories, opinions and ideas of several of the people present on any given occasion. Furthermore, there is no comparable expression of such an attitude to people with mental handicaps in Luther's own writings or in his vast public ministry. His critics would find themselves unable to produce evidence from any of the 110 volumes! Indeed there is a striking similarity between the accusations levelled against Luther and views attributed to another reformer, John Calvin. This suggests that unsubstantiated sources may have been copied by critics and applied to different people! If Luther really held to and taught such a wholly negative view of people with mental handicaps it is surprising that the Lutheran Church has shown such a positive attitude, particularly as exemplified at its Bethel village for people with handicaps during the reign of Nazi terror.

There is no doubt that Luther held that it is possible for people to be demon possessed—a view hardly likely to commend him, or Jesus Christ, to a twentieth-century agnostic. But of the association between mental handicap and demonisation there is insufficient evidence to hold Luther guilty!

The sixteenth century saw some progress in Christian understanding about mental handicap. A friend of Erasmus and Sir Thomas More, Juan Vives, initiated a plan for the city of Bruges for the compassionate treatment of people with mental handicaps, among others. This plan was embodied in English legislation in 1531 and 1536.

Meanwhile in Switzerland a distinction was being drawn between mental illness and mental handicap. This was being put forward by Paracelsus—he preferred not to use his own name of Aureolus Theophrastus Bombastus von Hohenheim, and who can blame him! He regarded people with mental handicaps as having more direct access to God than the rest of humanity, thus directly challenging the popular notion that demonisation must be the explanation of the differences. Certainly he acknowledged that 'fools' are as much human beings as any:

> Man's wisdom is nothing before God, but rather that all of us in our wisdom are like the fools. . . . Therefore the fools, our brethren, stand before us. . . . And he who redeemed the intelligent one, also redeemed the fool, as a fool. . . . even if the [physical] nature [of fools] went wrong, yet nothing has been wrong with the soul and the spirit.[7]

During this period it was common for people with mental handicaps to be used as 'fools' in rich, royal and even religious households. King Henry VIII and Cardinal Wolsey, Francis I of France and Pope Leo X all did so, the last keeping a group of people with physical and mental handicaps to provide entertainment for himself and his dinner party guests. Using them as figures of fun continued into the seventeenth century.

From 1600 to 1800

Legislation sometimes has unforeseen and unintended side-effects. This was certainly true of the Poor Laws which led to the setting up of workhouses. Increasing numbers of people with mental handicaps were confined for vagrancy, petty offences or bizarre behaviour. Effectively the institutionalisation of mentally handicapped people had begun. By 1789 there were between 4,000 and 5,000 people living in workhouses because of mental illness or handicap. 'Care' was usually little more than containment and menial labour. One of the exceptions was St Peter's workhouse in Bristol which, in 1696, was providing separate care and treatment to 'pauper lunatics'. Such an unusual degree of compassion lends weight to the legend that the founder was church warden of St Philips and St James.

During this period changes were taking place which were to influence substantially the attitudes towards people with mental handicaps displayed during the nineteenth century. One was the Industrial Revolution. Its effects upon the way society functioned was radical. Rural cottage industries were overtaken as employers of labour by mechanised mills and factories. Previously people who were poor, sick, insane, or mentally handicapped were accommodated within their village communities. The factory system and the development of huge, impersonal urban areas lacked the closeness and flexibility required to cope with their needs.

In the churches change was also evident, not only because of population movement. The era of the Puritans was past, with its emphasis on the Bible and practical, compassionate, personal religion. Deism became popular to the point that almost every other view was excluded. A natural outflow of the rationalism of the Enlightenment, deism held that God had retired, disinterested, from his creation. He was no longer concerned to redeem or heal, but had left creation to run down. The idea arose of a great chain of being in which living things took their place according to their moral worth, from the highest intelligences to the animal kingdom. This strengthened the belief that savages, slaves, criminals and people regarded as mentally abnormal were akin to animals, devoid of reason and beyond the pale of humanity. As the authors of their own misfortune (!) they must be corrected by brutalising discipline. The animality of people with mental disorders is a prominent theme in the eighteenth and nineteenth centuries, well reflected in the regular attendance of vast numbers of the public at Bethlem lunatic asylum for public entertainment—and the fact that the asylum lacked a chapel.

Madhouses were usually private dwellings, often run by

medical men or clergymen. The stereotype of these places and of the hospitals is one of harsh abuse of the inmates, with chains, bleedings, whippings and duckings unchanged since the Middle Ages. Care should be taken not to pass judgement on this without taking account of the harshness and squalor of contemporary life generally. Even these methods were sometimes well meant!

An example of an institution with church connections is Ireland's first hospital for the care of idiots and the insane. Jonathan Swift, better known for his satirical works such as *Gulliver's Travels*, was Dean of St Patrick's Anglican Cathedral in Dublin. He founded the hospital out of a concern at the lack of care for such people, and bequeathed to it the whole of his estate.

Swift's contemporary, Daniel Defoe, author of *Robinson Crusoe*, published plans for the building of a hospital for people with mental handicaps which reflect a relatively enlightened view of mental handicap. Defoe refers to Bethlem's original foundation as laudable but condemned its current use as entertainment.

Perhaps they [the inmates] are a particular rent-charge on the great family of mankind, left by the Maker of us all, like a younger brother, who though the estate be given from him, yet his father expected the heir should take some care of him.[8]

He argues for the appointment of a chaplain for both staff and residents, since God has through prayer restored reason to idiots. Providence brought this about 'perhaps among other wise ends, to confute that sordid supposition that idiots have no souls'. He spoke out against the custom of confining sane people for convenience sake.

If they are not mad when they go into these cursed houses they are soon made so by the barbarous usage they suffer. . . . Is it not enough to make anyone mad to be suddenly clapped up, stripped, whipped, ill fed and worse used?[9]

His complaints added fuel to the reform movement which led to the regulating of madhouses.

Hannah More was a pioneer of Sunday schools and close friend of William Wilberforce and the Clapham Sect. She took responsibility for a young woman with mental handicap found living rough near Bristol in 1781. Miss More sent her to a private asylum, probably against the girl's wishes, and on her decline into 'helpless idiocy' placed her in the lunatic wing of Guy's Hospital where she continued to pay for her keep and then for her funeral expenses on her death in 1800.

Across Europe the eighteenth century ended with optimism at man's potential and dignity. This proved a great stimulus to those who were beginning more clearly to draw the line between mental illness and mental handicap. In France the experiments of Jean Itard with the wild boy of Aveyron, Victor, drew wide interest.

In Britain Quakers such as Elizabeth Fry made a major contribution towards creating awareness of people with mental disorders in the course of her campaign for prison reform. In an 1827 report on the conditions of Irish prisons and workhouses there is an illuminating section focusing attention on the plight of the mentally ill and mentally handicapped people found incarcerated there. They were not usually guilty of criminal acts and often lived in bad conditions. Mrs Fry criticised the lack of congregational worship for this group and advocated religious teaching, Protestant or Catholic, for inmates generally. She mentioned the importance of the Bible, the need for the influence of the Holy Spirit and for belief in the Redeemer so that prisoners might 'obtain mastery over their evil passions'.

Another Quaker, Edward Wakefield, used his wide travels as a land agent to investigate madhouses. Bethlem's notoriety was to feature yet again when Wakefield reported on his visits there to the 1815 Select Committee investigating madhouses.

In the men's wing in the side room, six patients were chained close to the wall, five handcuffed . . . all were naked, except as

to the blanket gown or a small rug on the shoulders, and without
shoes. . . . The patients in this room, except the noisy one, and
the poor lad with cold feet, who was lucid when we saw him,
were dreadful idiots; their nakedness and mode of confinement
gave this room the complete appearance of a dog kennel. . . .[10]

Quakers were not only to the fore in campaigning but also
in providing for people with mental disorders. Edward Fox
ran a model asylum near Bristol, mainly for people who were
mentally ill. William Tuke founded the York Retreat, again
primarily for people with mental illness. Tuke, a tea and
coffee merchant, was stirred to concern when a friend died
in mysterious circumstances in York Asylum. What he saw
on visiting the asylum resulted in the opening of the retreat
in 1796. Here a small proportion of residents were admitted
on the grounds of their mental handicap and received devoted
attention, painstakingly recorded in case notes.

The regime in Tuke's asylum was in marked contrast to
that which he had seen in York. Patients were never
punished. Mechanical restraints were forbidden. An appeal
to the better side of the patient's nature was always made in
difficult situations. Religion was believed to aid recovery
through regular meetings, Bible readings, Bible study and
conversations with visiting Friends. In selecting staff, Tuke
looked among Friends for 'one who knows experimentally
the religion of the heart'.

Three evangelical men concerned about lunacy reform
were associated with the Clapham Sect. This was a group of
Christians noted for their combination of evangelical zeal
and social reform. William Wilberforce, its leader, spared
time from his campaign against slavery to serve on the
committee investigating the state of provision for 'pauper
lunatics'. Two other friends, William Smith MP and Lord
Robert Seymour, were active in the long-running battle to
reform provision for people with mental illness or mental
handicaps. In the course of their campaign Seymour visited
and reported on Warburton's madhouse in Bethnal Green:

There was a little hesitation in showing us the place . . . we found
a considerable number of very disgusting objects . . . chiefly
idiots, in a very small room; they were sitting on benches round
the room and several of them were chained to the wall. The air
of the room was highly oppressive and offensive, insomuch that
I could not draw my breath.[11]

After nearly fifteen years they saw the passing of the 1828
Act to regulate madhouses in London, which included a
requirement that divine worship should be performed every
Sunday.

It was during the passage of this Bill that Lord Shaftesbury
comes into the story, since it was in support of it that he
made his maiden speech in Parliament. He too was associated
with the Clapham Sect and had served on the Select Committee
which had investigated the state of madhouses. Having heard
the accounts of other eye witnesses, he decided to see for
himself what was going on in the semi-rural suburb of Bethnal
Green.

'I well remember,' he told the House of Commons many years
later, 'the sounds that assailed my ear and the sights that shocked
my eye' as he went round 'that abode of the most wretched'. He
was moved to the depths and returned home raging at the cruelty
and pain; the sufferings of his fellowbeings tore at his own nerves.
Yet Dr Warburton, who owned several other pauper madhouses
. . . was not a bad man at heart, merely struggling to earn his
living. After the Select Committee's findings he put his affairs in
order and spent liberally.[12]

In later years Shaftesbury was able to commend him publicly.
It is clear that Shaftesbury wanted to show the public that
neither mentally ill nor mentally handicapped people were
any longer to be shut out of sight as objects of disgust. Not
only should mental disorder be accommodated separately
from other conditions, but a further distinction should be
drawn by making particular provision for people with mental
handicaps. Shaftesbury's devotion to this cause spread over

nearly sixty years of public life, during most of which he was chairman of the Metropolitan Commissioners for Lunacy. He undertook regular visiting to asylums on Sundays—of which he wrote, 'There is nothing poetical in this duty, but every sigh prevented and every pang subdued is a song of harmony to the heart.'[13]

The honour for establishing Britain's first important provision for the care and training of people with mental handicaps must go to the Revd Andrew Reed (1787–1862). He was for fifty years the minister of Wycliffe Chapel, a Congregational church in London's East End. His work for people with mental handicaps was motivated by a deep gratitude for God's grace and a desire to love and serve him.

Reed's awareness of the needs of people with mental handicaps was aroused by a church member. Having already established three orphanages, he was asked to find help for her mentally handicapped son. He corresponded with some of the leading activists in the field of mental handicap in his day and visited the continent to see what was being done by way of care and training in France, Germany, Denmark and Switzerland. This confirmed his decision to set up similar provision in England.

With the help of others, some of whom were ministers, and in the presence of the Mayor of London, he launched The Society to Found a National Asylum for Idiots in 1847. By the following year it had opened a home in Highgate for fifty residents. A branch was opened at Essex Hall, Colchester, the following year. In 1855 the residents of the first house were transferred to a new asylum near Redhill, with Queen Victoria as its patron. It was to become known as the Royal Earlswood Hospital.

Reed was involved with the institutions, not only in the details of planning, management and selection of staff but with frequent visits and close personal contact with those who lived there. He ate with the children, took an interest in their enthusiasm for a pet rabbit, for sprouting seed and for the latest addition to the aviary.

Both of the institutions have continued to the present day, but the legacy of Reed's work is wider than their subsequent history. Breaking with past neglect, his work gave impetus for a succession of similar institutions, all carried on the tide of optimism about the capacity and value of people with mental handicaps. The return of people to the community was one of his objectives, with the intent that they should have meaningful lives and employment, but due to public attitudes this proved largely unattainable.

His efforts also raised the level of public concern on the subject and led to the passing of the Idiocy Act in 1866. It embodied a distinction on which he had insisted between mental illness and mental handicap. His institutions also became renowned as centres of research.

Perhaps the most instructive aspects of Andrew Reed's work, however, are his attitude to people with mental handicaps and the ethos of the institutions he built for them. He intended that Christian love should rule. He was concerned that the individuals should enjoy spiritual life.

Thank God, I have no satisfaction in labouring, even for the idiot, on mere temporal grounds. I must look at the soul, assist its development, point it to God and hope for its salvation.[14]

The Essex Hall asylum founded by Reed closed after only eight years due to lack of funds. An enthusiastic evangelical clergyman, the Revd Edwin Sidney, campaigned and collected for three years to reopen it. He too combined administration with close personal supervision. Sidney regarded the compassionate care and training of people with mental handicaps, which included both social skills and formal education, as a natural and pressing consequence of biblical Christianity—an absolute Christian duty. The idiot's 'case gave to Christians the opportunity of exercising the graces of the Gospel, and the responsibility of his condition rested with us upon whom God had made him dependent'. Bible teaching was at the heart of this, arising from a fervent desire that 'they be brought to know and acknowledge that Saviour which they had in common with ourselves'.[15]

By the end of the century the earlier optimism had given way to negative attitudes. The grand experiment seemed to have failed—education and training had not had the normalising effect anticipated. Once consigned to an institution, few emerged to take their place again in the community.

> The original asylums were never conceived of as life-long institutions, rather as places where idiots could be trained for a period of years, for as long as they made visible progress. However, there was often nowhere for idiots to return to . . . however well trained. And sometimes the expected improvements did not materialise. Under such conditions of increasing admissions and life-long residence, the asylums changed.[16]

Howe, a leading American humanitarian reformer campaigning from the mid-nineteenth century, promoted the view that idiocy was a symptom of social evils.

> The moral to be drawn from the existence of idiocy in society is that a very large class of persons ignore the conditions upon which health and reason are given to men, and consequently they sin in various ways.[17]

The evil of parental sins was to be atoned for by idiocy in the children. Howe particularly attacked alcoholism. Some writers attacked rising feminism!

The influence of Darwinism had persuaded the popular mind that mental handicap was a regression. People with mental handicaps ought to be segregated lest they multiply and thus lead to the degeneration of the race. Such thinking is reflected in the prospectus of a large hospital in about 1910:

> The Institutions are for permanent as distinct from temporary care, and no case is knowingly received as a temporary measure. Mentally defective persons of both sexes never acquire self-control, or become fit to cope on equal terms with normal people;

they remain children all their lives. . . . But it is important to remember that these same people turned out into the world to fend for themselves would at once cease to do any useful work. Not only would they fail to support themselves, but they would extort from the community the most expensive form of support as criminals and paupers.[18]

It is astonishing that this statement was approved by the founder of the hospital, the Revd Harold Burden, an ex-missionary with an interest in the spiritual care of his patients. Nor is there any evidence that the church made any protest about the segregation, confinement and even forced sterilisation of people with mental handicaps during these decades.

This relatively brief overview of Christian responses to people with mental handicaps is not encouraging, generally reflecting the attitudes prevalent at the time. One would hope that in our more enlightened age a greater degree of concern might be evident. That has yet to appear! In this century too the response of the church to people with mental handicap is largely due to the initiatives of a few committed individuals, often against the tide of Christian opinion. We will do well to look at them more closely.

Notes

1 B. Stratford, *Down's Syndrome: Past, Present and Future* (Penguin: London, 1989), p 15.
2 J. Ryan and F. Thomas, *The Politics of Mental Handicap* (Free Association Books: London, 1991), p 85.
3 J. Taylor, *The Church and Mental Handicap: In Search of a History* (Unpublished paper: UK, 1991).
4 M. Foucault, *Madness in Civilisation* (Tavistock Publications: London, 1961), p vii.
5 R. Porter, *Mind Forged Manacles: A History of Madness in England from the Restoration to the Regency* (Atholone Press: London, 1987), p 18.
6 J. Taylor, *op cit*, pp 20–22. The conclusions in this section on

Luther are strongly supported by scholars of Luther and his work in Germany and the USA.

[7] P.F. Cranefield and W. Federn, *The Begetting of Fools: an annotated translation of Paracelsus'* De Generations Stultorum.

[8] D. Defoe, *An Essay upon Projects*, quoted by Taylor, *op cit*, p 30.

[9] *Ibid*, p 31.

[10] R. Hunter and I. Macalpine, *Three Hundred Years of Psychiatry 1535–1860* (Oxford University Press: Oxford, 1963), p 699.

[11] K. Jones Law, *Lunacy and Conscience 1744–1845* (Routledge, Kegan & Paul: London, 1955), p 135.

[12] J. Pollock, *The Poor Man's Earl* (Hodder & Stoughton: London, 1985), p 34.

[13] *Ibid*, p 35.

[14] K. Heasman, *Evangelicals in Action* (Geoffrey Bles: UK, 1962), p 417.

[15] Taylor, *op cit*, p 43.

[16] Ryan, *op cit*, p 98.

[17] Quoted in Ryan, *op cit*, p 103.

[18] Quoted by Taylor, *op cit*, p 44, from 'Objects of the Institutions, Stoke Park Hospital, Bristol'.

I am indebted to Jeremy Taylor in researching this topic for me. As is evident from the references above, his paper has been the foundation for my own work in this chapter. Thanks, Jeremy!

5
What's Happening Now?

The picture of the past is rather discouraging. It has to be said that, by and large, Christians have shown serious disregard for people with mental handicaps. But things are changing; not as quickly as one might like, but there is real improvement to be seen. It would help to put things into a more accurate perspective if we spent some time looking at the way things are today. By comparison with the past, the scene is promising.

It is impossible in this chapter to give a comprehensive survey of contemporary Christian involvement in the field of mental handicap. Much of what is happening is small scale and low key, unknown beyond the circles in which it is taking place. Some of what is happening is the result of natural Christian witness flowing out from the caring life of the individual towards a neighbour in the street or people with whom he works.

Many things that are happening are similar to each other: a small group in a Sunday school; a home run for a group of people with mental handicaps by a Christian couple who bought a larger house to accommodate them; regular visits to a mental handicap hospital to take a service or Bible study meeting—and so on. It would be monotonous to repeat scenes which are more or less identical.

And some Christians would prefer to carry on serving God among people with mental handicaps without attention being drawn to their efforts. Which is understandable and acceptable. So, what follows is a taste of what is happening. God only knows all the efforts being made, all the care being shown, all the patient ministry taking place for the benefit of people with mental handicaps. Those involved do not need a mention by me to validate their work!

The examples which make up this chapter have been selected to show how diverse is the contemporary Christian response to people with mental handicaps. Some initiatives have become large organisations; some show how people whose only 'qualification' was compassion have achieved a great deal. As you read you may occasionally be filled with admiration for a person. More often you might think to yourself, 'I could do that.'

Jean Vanier

Some readers may have been offended by the lack of reference to Roman Catholic provision for mentally handicapped people thus far. Sorry about that! It's not my scene and researching it would have been a huge task. In an attempt to redress that imbalance let me start this contemporary view by focusing on a Roman Catholic who has gained international recognition for his work with and for people with mental handicaps—Jean Vanier. By nationality he is French; he was born of French Canadian parents, educated in England, served with the British navy, and has lived the greater part of his life in France!

Jean Vanier is a devout Catholic whose faith in Jesus has determined his response to the needs of people with mental handicaps. His concern was stirred by Father Thomas when visiting France from Canada, where Vanier was a lecturer in ethics. In the 1960s this humble priest had moved into a village in France to live in poverty and to serve the poor. The village included a community of thirty-two men with mental handicaps to whom he became chaplain. Father Thomas spoke to Jean Vanier about the spiritual openness of handicapped people and suggested to him that there was 'something special to be done among handicapped people'.

Jean Vanier subsequently visited an institution near Paris where eighty men with mental handicaps lived in 'a chaotic atmosphere of violence and uproar'. The conviction grew with him that 'Jesus wanted something to be done'. In the summer of 1964 he bought a small house in Trosly-Breuil, the village where Father Thomas lived and worked. Three men with mental handicaps exchanged the chaos of the Paris institution for the quiet of Vanier's home. One could not cope and returned to the institution the next day. Jean and his new friends called their home L'Arche, the ark.

A few months later a crisis occurred in Val Fleuri, the institution in the village, when all but two of the staff resigned. Vanier was asked to take over as director. It was March 1965. The place was disturbed and disturbing, but with the help of a handful of professionals who volunteered their help, change began to take place. People were moved into new homes and others moved into the region to join them. By 1972 there were 126 residents living in 20 L'Arche homes in the Trosly-Breuil area.

The development of an international federation of L'Arche communities began in 1969 with a home in Canada. By the end of 1970 a home had opened in Bangalore, India, followed by others in four cities during the 1970s. Soon there were also homes in Africa and South America. Often they followed visits by Jean Vanier to take retreats. There are now about ninety communities in twenty-two countries.

L'Arche is a very diverse movement. Its communities all seek to function as places where assistants live with people with mental handicaps. Long-term members of the communities 'announce a covenant' with God and with the residents. The communities reflect the religion and culture of the countries in which they are set. In France they display Vanier's Catholic roots, while in England they take a more Anglican profile. In India the majority of residents and assistants are Hindus, with some Muslims. This presents some difficulties in viewing the organisation as a specifically Christian work.

Another aspect of Vanier's work has been the establishing of the Faith and Light movement. This now encompasses 750 groups in over 50 countries. They meet regularly for prayer, sharing and celebration, drawing together mentally handicapped people, their friends and families.

In the church at large few people have done as much as Jean Vanier to encourage the acceptance of people with mental handicaps. While respecting and admiring this, many non-Catholics will be uncomfortable with some of his emphases. Seeing virtue in poverty actually inhibits the recognition of people with mental handicaps as one with us. His emphasis on spirituality is welcome, but the multi-faith mysticism embraced causes confusion as to what spirituality is. It undercuts the Bible he obviously respects and draws upon. But let it be unreservedly acknowledged that few of us will ever come near him in the good he has brought into the lives of countless numbers of people with mental handicaps!

Walsingham Community Homes

Walsingham Community Homes is quite different in scale and origin. It began life in a Roman Catholic centre and is now based in the same building as the education department of the Methodist Church, a fitting illustration of the ecumenical thrust of the organisation. 'Walsingham' is a relatively recent development of Christian concern for people with mental handicaps, and one which has grown with impressive speed.

As with many initiatives in Christian circles, this story starts with an individual. Mark Snell was successful as a travel agent, running his own business. He was content to pursue the priority of his contemporaries—to make money. Then he discovered that his son Matthew had a mental handicap, a discovery which changed his outlook and challenged his priorities. He decided to take up work with people with disabilities, but it was an ambition he found difficult to fulfil. His only experience was as a parent of a person with a mental handicap!

After three years' searching he found the sort of job he wanted. It was with St Joseph's Centre, a Roman Catholic base encouraging friendship and support for people with mental handicaps in the churches of the diocese of Westminster. Parents attending the centre expressed a common anxiety: 'Who will care for my child when I'm gone?' And they added another question: 'What will the church do about it?' As Mark pursued the issue he found that at first the parents saw the solution as increasing the number of institutions. When questioned more closely, some common themes began to appear: small homes; ordinary houses; not far from the family; Christian homes where the local church would provide a welcoming community.

The next approach was made to the headquarters of the main denominations. 'In your churches do you have parents who face this problem?' Mark asked. 'Yes,' was the answer. 'What is the answer for those parents?' he questioned. 'Don't know,' was the reply. 'Will you give moral support to find an answer?' 'Rather!' they said. Mark pondered the issue, and it was actually while he was at Walsingham, a shrine dedicated to Christian unity, that he came up with a solution.

An organisation was formed, eventually called Walsingham Community Homes, to develop homes to be supported ecumenically wherever they were opened and to be staffed by professing Christians. The first was opened in Watford in 1987. By March 1992 there were 22 homes caring for 118 residents representing a wide range of handicaps and disabilities. Most of the residents have been resettled from long-stay mental handicap hospitals. More are now coming from family settings.

The pace of development reflects an opportunist approach on Mark's part. He saw the possibility of providing Christian homes now, and feared that failure to respond would result in permanently lost ground. He was determined to ensure a

Christian presence among those who provide care for people with mental handicaps.

However, most of the residents come from the secular environment of an institution, with little experience of Christian values. Developing a Christian ethos while employing staff with a wide diversity of Christian backgrounds is a challenge. The fundamental demonstration of Christian care is expressed in the values in the homes, in seeing people as equals and relating as friends. And it gets through to many of the folk who live in the homes.

Tony lived in a Walsingham home for only fifteen months before his death. He attended the parish church and touched the people in the area by his presence. He would iron shirts for neighbours for 25 pence a go. At his funeral 300 people attended to express their respect for him.

The Lodge Trust

For Fred Hutton teacher training college was a life-changing experience. While a student he became a Christian, and this in turn opened up a new dimension to his studies. A series of lectures on special needs education also gave them a new direction. On leaving college he became a teacher of children with special needs and then, after further study, a polytechnic lecturer training teachers of children with mental handicaps.

His settled world at Loughborough was disturbed by a story in the local newspaper about a new project to build a village in rural Leicestershire for people with mental handicaps. What caught his eye was the fact that, during his years as a teacher, he had taught the son of the man behind the venture. Fred became involved and, in 1973, was appointed to head up the project to establish the village on a green field near Shangton. It would house fifty people with mental handicaps plus live-in staff, and provide workshops and a village centre. This local venture was linked to a national organisation, then still relatively small, called Cottage And Rural Enterprises— CARE.

Five years later, with Shangton established, Fred Hutton found himself with new responsibilities following the sudden death of the founder of CARE. Fred took on the national responsibility for the caring work of the organisation. During his time in that role the number of villages grew to 6, with approximately 200 residents in all. That growth brought management, administration and travel in plenty as villages were opened in Northumbria, Kent and Lancashire—villages already existed in Devon, Leicestershire and Sussex.

Inevitably Fred had less contact with people with mental handicaps, which he missed. He also found himself having more contact with Christian families who wanted a home where their sons or daughters could continue to enjoy a way of life compatible with their beliefs. This led him to consider setting up a home of his own where he would be free to operate within a framework which more fully expressed his own faith. In the autumn of 1983 he bought The Lodge, a beautiful stone-built house standing on the edge of Market Overton in Rutland. Within a few months it had been transformed into a welcoming home for the first of its ten residents. Subsequently a further cottage has been built in the grounds to accommodate ten more people with mental handicaps. Along the way 'The Lodge' became a registered charitable trust, spending over £750,000 provided in answer to prayer.

Fred Hutton is a firm believer in what used to be called 'the Protestant work ethic'. He sees the development of work skills as deeply therapeutic for people with a mental handicap. It provides a framework for the day and enables them to serve others as well as enhancing their own life. The work will be most satisfying if it has an end product which reflects well on the person doing the work. Any buyer will be happy to purchase the item because of its inherent value, not as an act of charity.

This philosophy has shaped activities at The Lodge. Extensive horticultural work takes place in the grounds and greenhouses. The houses are supplied with most of the fruit and vegetables they require. Jam- and pickle-making takes place in the kitchen, turning garden produce into a very popular line for the annual open day sale. Workshops produce wooden toys and other goods to a high standard. A variety of other crafts are taught. In the evenings a number of classes are run by volunteers on topics as varied as needlework and healthy eating.

A Christian view of life pervades everything that happens at The Lodge. Staff and residents join in 'family prayers' daily. Twice a month it includes an afternoon service to which local people are welcome, providing an occasion when people can share their faith in worship of God, regardless of their abilities or disabilities.

ARK

So far we have looked at what can happen when one person responds to the needs of people with mental handicaps. It is time to look at what can happen when a church responds to the needs of one person with a mental handicap. The congregation of Morningside Baptist Church in Edinburgh could not have known what would flow from the minister's remark one Sunday morning in 1976.

Many of the people released from mental handicap hospitals in the 1970s and 1980s should never have been there in the first place. Strictly speaking they did not have a mental handicap, but they did have difficulty coping with the demands and complexities of life. Katie was one such. She had lived in a mental handicap hospital in Edinburgh until her brother secured her discharge so that she could care for their dying mother. After the funeral Katie returned to Edinburgh, expecting to enter the secure environment of the hospital. Instead she found there was no longer a place for her.

Living in the community, she went from digs to bed-sits; from one short-term job to another, barely coping with life on her own outside of the institution which had trained her to be dependent. Katie also discovered church—Morningside

Baptist Church, to be precise. There she was welcomed and befriended, even when she switched her radio on during the sermon! Her personal situation deteriorated and her frustrations were increasingly expressed towards the very people who had shown her love. Peter Bowes, the minister, had one very trying week as a result of Katie's activities. On the Sunday morning in question he shared his concern for her with the congregation and suggested an impromptu meeting afterwards for those who would like to help her. A group of fifteen or so, mainly professionals of one sort or another, met in the vestry and formed a working group, unsure of what they could do but committed to doing something. Their early enquiries were fruitful and led to the formation the following year of the first specialist housing association in Scotland for people with mental handicaps.

One of the couples involved, Norman and Ruth Middleton, made their dining room the headquarters of the embryonic organisation. From there the first home was planned by the working group, opening in Edinburgh in 1979. There were ten residents with two and a half staff (!)—all that was possible within the funding at that time.

The housing association was named ARK because of the biblical connotation. It suggests a permanent place of refuge and shelter for the disadvantaged person, within which he or she can make as much contribution as he or she is able. The Christian origins of the association have shaped its philosophy. This is expressed in three basic principles:
—Christian compassion expressed by love, care and concern, illustrated by the teaching and commands of Jesus Christ;
—community responsibility in that the local community should be involved in the setting up and continued running of the projects;
—all residents and tenants with a mental handicap share the same basic needs, rights and responsibilities, have the same human value, and are entitled to the same consideration and respect as other people in society.

From its early and uncertain beginnings, ARK has grown

to become a major provider of a range of supported accommodation for people with mental handicaps in many regions of Scotland. Its tenants include some people who, though having handicaps, are able to cope with independence; some require support for daily living; and some with multiple handicaps require relatively high levels of staff care. The first community house ARK opened was what one would expect for such a project in the late 1970s—it was housed in a former nursing home. Since then the diversity of housing has increased considerably. At Macduff, for example, the association has built a small estate where some houses are let to tenants from the local authority's housing list, while some houses are let to tenants who have mental handicaps. Earlier community houses now have satellite houses. There are now over 25 local groups supporting projects which care for a total of about 300 residents.

The demands of such growth have led to the association widening its employment to include people who are not necessarily Christians. However, everyone involved must affirm their agreement to the objective of the organisation: 'ARK's prime objective is the development of housing models which fully reflect Christian concern in supporting the whole person, physical, mental and spiritual.' What an outcome from practical concern for one person in need!

Moorfield House

Joan and David Lamkin seemed to have no particular reason for opening a home for people with mental handicaps. Even now there is an element of surprise when they look back over the steps which led to Moorfield House. Theirs was a private family, involved in running their own business and active in their local church. But they were not unaware of people in need.

For Joan, contact with 'difficult children' had been part of her upbringing. Her parents had regularly fostered children in need. It was quite natural that she and David should become long-term foster parents for Jane, a girl with multiple handicaps. Arranging this brought them into contact with Barnardo's, who previously had cared for Jane. That in turn drew their attention to the fact that many young people with handicaps faced a bleak future when they reached nineteen years of age.

Almost without realising it, these factors were pointing David and Joan in a new direction. Increasingly they found their thoughts turning to ways in which they could make some response to people with mental handicaps. Their first enquiries about residential care, sometime in 1983, were ill-timed due to bad publicity for independent homes in the Southport area. However, the idea would not go away and increasingly they felt drawn towards specific action. Early in 1985 they renewed contact with the registration officer of the social services department and found, to their surprise, that an invitation was on its way to a meeting for people wanting to become more involved.

There followed a series of surprising incidents. Individually they might have been taken as coincidences, but together they marked out a pathway which the Lamkins saw as God's clear guidance for their lives. One sequence led them to Moorfield House in Melling, Merseyside. Its location, size and potential both excited and overawed them. At each stage they were able to move forward, in spite of opposition to their planning application. There were legal hurdles to overcome, financial requirements to be met and registration as a residential care home to be obtained. But as 1985 ended all was to hand and the first resident was in place.

The first task was to transform the house into a home suitably restored and furnished for twelve people. It was quite an undertaking, completed in sixteen weeks by dint of hard work. But this was by no means the whole story. There were also outbuildings crying out to be renovated and used. The barn was upgraded to provide for two groups of four people able to live semi-independently. The cottage was adapted for a further three. And a former Gospel Hall was moved from

Liverpool docks to provide a recreation room. Having by this time ensured a high standard of care for people with mental handicaps, the Lamkins themselves moved out of the main house into a bungalow in the grounds. It was as if, by this action, the whole venture had come to maturity!

The hallmark of Moorfield House is commitment to care arising from the personal experience of God of those who work there. The residents have benefited enormously from their new environment. All have come from family settings rather than institutions, and are all in their twenties or thirties.

Barely ten years passed between the fostering of Jane and the final stage of development at Moorfield House. So much happened in that period that it is difficult for those involved to believe it could have happened in such a relatively short time. Even the Lamkins are not sure they have arrived!

The legacy of Lord Shaftesbury

At first glance it is surprising that, during the nineteenth century, when now-famous societies were being formed to meet a range of social needs, no organisation emerged to champion the cause of people with mental handicaps. This may in part be because the institutions were seen as 'the solution'. It may also be because the scale of human need was vast and the resources of the responding charities were limited.

As the twentieth century passed its mid-point, those older societies were increasingly responsive to the needs of children and adults with mental handicaps. Today, for example, Barnardo's, National Children's Homes, The Children's Society and the Shaftesbury Society are among organisations operating a variety of schemes. They bring to the task the wealth of their long experience in providing care for disadvantaged people, the maturity of established management structures, the resources of numerous supporters and their considerable reputations. The number and diversity of projects established during the past twenty years is enormous. To

sample this diversity we will look more closely at the
contribution of the Shaftesbury Society.

During the nineteenth century Lord Shaftesbury had a
profound impact on social needs. The Ragged Schools Union,
with his support, became renowned throughout the world for
its educational and caring work for people with physical
disabilities, the more so after it was renamed after its famous
leader. In Christian circles the Society gained a reputation
for its mission work in deprived 'inner city' areas of London.

In the 1980s two factors drew the Society into the field of
mental handicap. There was a growing awareness of the needs
of people with mental handicaps, and an increased opportunity
to respond to those needs as a result of changes in regulations
governing the Society's housing association. The trigger for
moving from awareness to active provision was provided by
a minister in Harlow. The Revd Jos Smith had become
involved with people with mental handicaps locally and
established a club for them. This had led to his setting up a
hostel. Jos Smith approached the Shaftesbury Society about
the possibility of their taking responsibility for the David
Livingstone Hostel. The time—1982—was right! The speed
of the developments which have followed is astonishing.

Two years later the first hostel was built in Islington and
opened the following year. 'Trueloves' in Essex, a one-time
residential school for children with physical disabilities, was
reopened as a home for people with mental handicaps. In
1985 a shared housing scheme was ready for people with
mental handicaps or physical disabilities. In 1986 the David
Livingstone Hostel was replaced with a new home, Livingstone
House, and a housing complex was built in Beckton to include
a home for people with mental handicaps.

By the beginning of 1992 the Shaftesbury Society was
providing care for about 220 people with mental handicaps
in 13 centres. Some are for people living more or less
independently in flats. A group of ten people live in a row
of five terraced houses on the South coast, receiving different
levels of support from staff as required. Some centres provide

for people who need a high level of care due to multiple handicaps.

Many of the residents have come into the care of the Society from long-stay mental handicap hospitals. Four elderly ladies in one home have each spent over sixty years in institutions. One of them, now over eighty, has no concept of retirement as she attends everything on offer, as if doing her utmost to make up for lost years.

Staff in the Society are required to accept and function within the clear Christian principles of the organisation. It seeks to provide Christian care by means of a 'quality service' which respects the value of each person. Good relationships are encouraged, helping people to grow, to choose and to mature. Indeed the Society hopes that maturity will result in an increasing number of people moving into their own independent accommodation, while retaining the support of staff if they need it.

In spite of this strong Christian ethos there is frequently a reluctance on the part of local churches to get involved with residents who attend their church. Not, however, in all cases. At Livingstone House, for example, strong links have been forged by several residents with the nearby Baptist church. Staff from the home have run a training course for church members who wish to show themselves welcoming and supportive. A fortnightly Causeway Bible group takes place on church premises, run by staff from the home. It is attended by local people with mental handicaps as well as some residents from Livingstone House.

Two members from the church visit Livingstone House twice a week in the late evening to read the Bible and pray with three residents who have asked for help in this way. How pleased God must be to see this happening!

In the churches

In 1990 there were nearly 51,000 churches in the United Kingdom.[1] It would be presumptuous to attempt in a few lines to say what they are, or are not, doing about people with mental handicaps. Without question many churches are trying to respond to the needs around them in various ways and with varying degrees of success. It is time to look at some of what is happening within the main denominations and to focus more closely on one or two particular examples of what local churches have achieved.

By the nature of the case denominations are large and cumbersome organisations. They respond to enormous diversity within the numerous congregations associated with them, reflecting differences in culture, theology, and tradition. It is far from easy to find out what is happening at the various levels of their church and organisational life.

To make it that much more difficult, some denominations have no particular group or committee which focuses specifically on mental handicap. For instance, the Methodist Church seeks to cover the issue within its Family, Healing and Personal Concerns Committee. That, in turn, reports to the Division of Social Responsibility. It is not surprising that such a group finds itself overwhelmed with the enormous range of issues it faces. Within the United Reformed Church mental handicap is part of the brief of the Faith and Light department. At the time of writing, the Salvation Army has a Fellowship of Endeavour which works to cultivate a right attitude to people with all forms of disability, but no ministry specifically targeted on people with mental handicaps.

Then there are the denominations which are so vast that their substructures allow for regional bodies of considerable size and power. In the Anglican Church the local scene may reflect the particular interests of the bishop concerned. Thus it is impossible to form a picture of what the Church of England is doing nationally. In the diocese of Winchester a research project in 1991 found that the majority of churches (66 per cent) included mentally disabled people in their congregation.[2]

In the diocese of Liverpool mental handicap has been the focus of an active subcommittee of the Board of Social

Responsibility. The group has run day retreats on the subject and a resource centre for clergy, with numerous books and other aids. Sister Ruth Reed, a diocesan worker, produced a *Confirmation Pack For Those With Learning Disabilities*, published by the Church Army in 1990. As a result of the group's activities there is a higher profile for mental handicap issues in the churches.

The Roman Catholic Church is similarly very diverse, frustrating any attempt to give a simple summary of its contribution in this field of activity. It has long-standing institutions for people with mental handicaps. Its Pope and bishops have often spoken of the needs of those whom society marginalises. One shining example in Britain of their contribution has been the work of the St Joseph's Pastoral Centre. It undertook pioneer work in preparing children with mental handicaps for confirmation. It produces resources for clergy to use in taking individuals through the catechism. It encourages the development of support and befriending groups. It has initiated retreats for people with mental handicaps. In fact it has done everything possible to bring them within the orbit of what is normal for a practising Catholic. Much of its work has become a pattern for others to follow way beyond the diocese of Westminster which established the centre.

A Baptist working group on mental handicap was established in the early 1980s. Now known as BUILD—The Baptist Union Initiative on people with Learning Disabilities—it has done a great deal to raise awareness within the denomination. Members of the group have been campaigners for the acceptance of people with mental handicaps. They have spoken at numerous meetings in churches and taken seminars in denominational theological colleges. Between them the members have written three books on the topic, including *Who's This Sitting In My Pew?* by Faith Bowers. In 1991 they published three discipleship booklets for use with people with learning disabilities. In 1992 they held a theological consultation on mental handicap. And they publish a quarterly bulletin to keep the issue before ministers and members of Baptist churches. Without doubt their wide-ranging activities are having an effect.

The contribution of the Church of Scotland earns a special mention! In some respects it reflects a different way of doing things in Scotland, particularly in the field of education. One in a Hundred is a project of the education department of the denomination. It began as a modest initiative in the 1970s when a group was set up to consider how the Church of Scotland could help people with special educational needs. It is now a well established part of the church's response to this challenge, and has two full-time officers. Over the years it has developed resources to enable the ministers and members of the church to respond to people with mental handicap. Broadly speaking it works on three fronts.

Schools in Scotland—including special schools—have chaplains attached to them. The local Church of Scotland minister is likely to be one of them. One in a Hundred provides training courses for ministers who have this opportunity, thus enabling them to make their contribution really worthwhile.

One in a Hundred also helps churches to respond by providing an information pack about mental handicap. In addition to this it operates The Church Advisorate in Special Educational Needs—CASPEN for short. This is a team of specialists in mental handicap who have volunteered their help to churches to speak at meetings or give advice as needed.

People with mental handicaps are also provided for by the publication of *Walk in God's Ways*. This is a confirmation pack of nine core lessons, with two additional sessions as options. Along with a tape, songs and simplified Bible reading material this is an invaluable resource. Another pack is being prepared for use with people with profound disabilities. By such measures the full integration of people with mental handicaps is being positively encouraged.

In addition to this educational work the Church of Scotland

is also providing residential care for adults with mental handicaps. It provides care for seventy adults in six homes as well as running a home for children up to sixteen years of age. Many of the residents have come from institutions. In age and degrees of handicap there is considerable variety.

Although the homes are run by the Church of Scotland, residents are encouraged to attend the church of their choice and are supported in developing links with that church.

Kingsbridge

In the relatively quiet corner of south-west Devon, Kingsbridge Baptist Church has found itself drawn into responding to people with mental handicaps. The person who has 'led' this response is the assistant pastor, Graham Fish. I say 'led' with tongue in cheek because his first reaction to the possibility was less than positive!

> I looked at her, stunned by what she had said. All I could manage in reply was, 'OK, I'll think about it', swallowing a hard lump that had stuck in my throat. The lady I was talking to was the mother of Ian who lived at Gordon Carling Homes, one of the local Mencap homes in Kingsbridge. She had told me how much Ian enjoyed church and how people with a mental handicap needed to feel they belonged and were part of their local community. But what really stunned me was that she thought someone from the church should go and visit and get involved. And it seemed that person was me.

Graham had little or no prior personal contact with people with mental handicaps. He didn't know what to say to them or how to behave with them. And he wasn't at all keen to do as he was asked. But he did what he promised Ian's mother he would do: he prayed about it. Praying resulted in his going to see the manager of the home where Ian lived. The idea was to arrange for someone from the church to make a regular visit to the home—someone other than himself!

Graham and the manager met and chatted, then made a

tour of the complex. Graham felt uncomfortable; the residents were shy. The best he could manage in conversation was a timid, 'Hello.' There were awkward silences. On his way home Graham asked God to let him off this one, but he didn't. Wednesday afternoons from 4.30 to 5.00 pm were his times for calling in for a chat. The subjects ranged from work to food, from holidays to Mum. Graham was still tense and nervous because it took time to get used to conversations with long silences in them; it took weeks to understand everything that was said because the residents would pronounce words in ways he was unused to hearing. He would get embarrassed; they would get frustrated. Time and again Graham asked God for help—and it was given. Gradually friendships were made and Graham found himself seeing people with handicaps rather than handicapped people. Change in himself enabled him to see his friends as unique individuals, each special to God. The home helped by including him in the training programme for new staff.

Before long the residents of Gordon Carling Homes began attending services at Kingsbridge Baptist Church. One Sunday one of them took home a brochure about Spring Harvest and expressed an interest in attending. Others wanted to go too, so next spring Graham found himself leading a group of seven, plus helpers, to the Christian holiday conference at Butlin's in Minehead. That's where we met, as Graham and his friends attended the meetings which Madeleine and I were leading for people with mental handicaps.

It marked another stage for Graham, Alan, Rose and David, the key group in this developing awareness. They discovered that people with mental handicaps could become committed Christians, could pray and benefit from reading God's word. They saw how to communicate the gospel simply so as to teach truths and concepts to people who do not easily learn such things.

On returning to Kingsbridge the pace of involvement quickened. The home asked the church to run a weekly club for residents of local homes. About thirty people attended for games, snooker, and the like, concluding the evening with singing Christian songs. The next step was to set up a house group for those who wanted to know more about Jesus. A special service is held in mental handicap week in June. The church responded positively to a request to run a Gateway club for adults with mental handicaps. About sixty people attend.

Not surprisingly, the church now has a number of people with mental handicaps in its Sunday services. It is becoming more used to their presence. The members are no longer put off by their singing, nor do they feel uncomfortable with them as once they did. And a good deal has changed in the church as it has grappled with communicating the good news of Jesus to a diverse congregation made up of people without any Christian background, people on holiday, people with mental handicaps and, of course, the members of the church!

The challenge of Ian's mother has resulted in lasting good to a significant number of people. Graham's initially reluctant but positive response has had eternally positive consequences. For him and those who have shared his concern the effects have been life-changing!

Kingsbridge is not the only town blessed with a church alive to the spiritual needs of people with mental handicaps. They may not be common, but such churches exist in many other places. Like Haywards Heath, where a commitment to benefit people with mental handicaps has long been the concern of members of the evangelical church in New England Road. It began with their interest in people who were part of their congregation, one lady in particular whose mother was elderly. They intended to establish a home nearby where they could care for them. At times the dream looked as though it would become a reality, but it was not to be. Frustrated by local planners, or local protests, or local prices, all the efforts to find suitable property failed.

The woman for whom they were concerned moved into a residential care home. Members of the church developed links with the home, and in due course, a Causeway bible group was begun to provide Bible teaching and worship within the grasp, and relevant to, people with mental handi-caps. Many of its members attend the church on Sunday. From time to time church members welcome group members into their homes. Strong links have been forged with individuals and families.

And so on. What you have read in this chapter is, as already stated, only a sample of what is going on. If you expected a comprehensive survey you will have been disappointed, but that would require a book in its own right. Thankfully, so much is now happening that one would have to include many more examples like that of Graham Fish in Kingsbridge, or David and Joan Lamkin in Merseyside. The book would describe more fully the work that is going on quietly in denominational committees. There is a great deal going on, and it seems to be increasing.

To be thorough such a survey would also have to include the numerous Christians working with people and children with mental handicaps in education departments and special schools, in social services, in health authorities and in charities and voluntary organisations which do not take a specifically Christian stance. They are providing front-line commitment, expressing the warm love and care of God's heart for the disadvantaged.

But, when all is said and done, they are very few when compared with the enormous number of people with mental handicaps in our society.

A Cause for Concern

You will not, I trust, be either surprised or offended if I include a mention of A Cause for Concern in more detail than other organisations mentioned. That's because I know more about it, having been closely involved from the outset.

Though we were not aware of it, A Cause for Concern began for Madeleine and me on 13 August 1963. Two unusual things happened that day: our first child, Rachel, was born (which was unusual in the sense that having children doesn't happen frequently in one family); also, I was asked to become the minister of Little Ilford Baptist Church in East London. At the time I thought the second of these events was the most significant as it seemed to mark out our life's work. Important as it was, in due course it was to be eclipsed by the effect Rachel was to have in our lives. I have already described the events surrounding her birth and our discovery of her handicap.

As the years passed, Rachel began to use the 'special' services provided for children with mental handicaps. We joined organisations for parents and began to meet other families facing similar issues. We also noticed that many of the parents were much older than we were, and that quite elderly folk would be caring for an adult son or daughter. And we heard the question 'What is going to happen?' framed in various ways as parents expressed their anxiety about the future for their son or daughter.

Early in 1973 Madeleine and I began to look at the answers available to parents facing such questions. We were amazed to find that little was being done by anybody, and almost nothing by Christians—especially those from our own evangelical background. The more we enquired and reflected on the position, the more aware we were that something needed to be done. In November of that year an article by me was published in *The Evangelical Times* entitled 'A Cause for Concern'. It triggered a response among readers which, in due course, led to the setting up of Christian Concern for the Mentally Handicapped—the registered charity title of A Cause for Concern. The aim of the new organisation was to focus Christian concern for people with mental handicaps in ways which would support them and their families. At the outset the first concern was to provide long-term residential care.

At that early stage we understood little about mental handicap and even less about setting up and running homes. (It has to be admitted that it would be almost impossible to do now what was done then because of the greater degree of government regulation and control of residential care homes.) We were prepared to do what we believed God was leading us to do, and we trusted him to provide the resources we would need to do it.

The first possibility of establishing a home occurred in Aberystwyth. The members of Alfred Place Baptist Church were aware of the need because two of their families had a mentally handicapped child. A home committee was formed to work with the charity to buy and open a home in the town. Eventually a suitable property was identified and negotiations began over the price. In due course it was agreed that we should pay £38,000 for Plas Lluest, an imposing mansion standing in about six acres of land on a hill overlooking the town and the bay. The price looks small today, but there was less than £4,000 in the bank at the time.

The development of Plas Lluest took years to achieve—buying it was an almost two-year process, and refurbishing it took nearly three years. But late in 1979 the first of the sixteen residents for whom it was to become home, moved in. Being the charity's first home, people came from far and near to live there. Carolyn came from Bristol, Andy from Southampton, Tim from Oxford, Richard from London—and some came from Wales.

By this time two other significant steps had been taken. In 1978 a home committee was set up in Dorset, linked to the Central Evangelical Church in Corfe Mullen. It was the culmination of concern on the part of a group of Christian parents to see a suitable home for their sons in that area.

The other step was more unexpected. In May 1979 a terrace of houses came on the market in Reading, to be auctioned in July. The houses had formerly been an old people's home. A series of miracles led to the charity being able to buy the houses for £85,000. With the help of members and friends of Carey Baptist Church, Helena House was converted over the next two years to become a home for eighteen people, this time drawn from a less extensive area.

The early 1980s were full of activity. In 1982 both Jireh House in Maidstone and Helena House in Reading opened for residents. What was to become Marion House was purchased in Bournemouth, and Birchwood was bought in Deganwy.

By the end of 1985 there were forty people living in homes run by A Cause for Concern. In 1986 Marion House opened for a further eight people. Plans had been approved for the home on vacant land behind the new church building at Bayston Hill near Shrewsbury. And another project had been added near Oswestry—on the Quinta estate in Weston Rhyn. We were to prepare two bungalows as a home for two groups of six people. Delays meant that carefully planned and phased development actually took place at the same time in 1988. To add to the feeling of disorganisation, it was also when two new houses were being built for the charity in the grounds of Plas Lluest.

A year later York House in Bayston Hill began to provide care for ten people, Perry Lodge and Reed House on the Quinta were fully operational, and numbers 1 and 2 Hafen-y-Coed at Plas Lluest were up and running. Then in 1990 two houses were bought in Lisburn, opening in 1991 and 1992.

More could be said about buildings and projects. It is the people who are really important. At the time of writing, the charity provides care and day services for eighty people with mental handicaps. Some spent as much as twenty-five years in institutions before coming into the charity's care. Some came from their caring Christian family. Some were referred by their social services department. Not all have stayed with us. A few have found it impossible to settle. There have been instances where parents have missed their son or daughter so much that he or she has had to return to the family home. And some have grown old or ill and died—how they have been missed.

What changes we have seen in people. Some who came so thoroughly institutionalised that they could not switch on the light are now able to play their part in their home. Some who could hardly speak have become articulate. Some who could not dress themselves have learned to do so. It is not simply a matter of new skills being learned but of the development of self-awareness and self-confidence. Most have grown in self-respect and dignity.

The Christian philosophy of the charity has been applied to every aspect of its work. Its attitude to people with mental handicaps has its roots in the Bible—and is more fully worked out in other chapters of this book. All staff are practising Christians—and over the years that has been the cause of some shortages as vacancies have been hard to fill. The standard of support and care in the homes is of a high order, yet must not undermine the individual's development. And the relationships encouraged are those described in the New Testament, where love for one another is the hallmark of real care.

The most exciting expression of this took place in 1992 when the first charity conference was held. Everybody involved in the organisation was invited. One hundred people, residents and staff, spent three days in a residential conference enjoying and participating in everything as equals. The theme, 'Serve each other with love', expressed the ethos of the event.

Financial policy also reflects the Christian stance of the organisation. Frequently it has been the case that the charity has launched a project convinced that it was what God wanted it to do, yet not having to hand the resources required to complete the task. It would not be true to say that this has always been straightforward. At times it seemed that the charity staggered from one financial crisis to another, with the bank murmuring that the condition was terminal! But it is true to say that, over the years, God has provided all the money needed for the tasks undertaken, and the homes continue to provide a high level of care and support for the residents.

Alongside of the exciting growth in residential and day services something else was taking place quietly. It began in the most ordinary way. One typical Sunday morning, probably in early 1983, Madeleine and I were sitting in church behind a row of people with mental handicaps. The sermon was being preached 'faithfully', but not interestingly enough to stop Madeleine wondering what the people in front of us were gaining from the 'message'. That in turn led to her setting up a Bible group for the residents of Helena House in Reading. After about three years the group began to hold its fortnightly meeting in a town centre location so that other people with mental handicaps could more easily attend. Gradually more and more joined the group. The numbers became so large that it divided into four groups.

During a visit to Spring Harvest we observed that several people with mental handicaps attended, so we suggested that some ministry should be provided that would take account of their limitations and needs. (Spring Harvest is a Christian holiday conference which takes place each Easter in Butlin's holiday villages.) We ran a week of seminars for people with mental handicaps for a week at the Minehead venue in 1986. Attendance was twenty-four people. The following year we ran a week at Minehead and another at the Skegness venue. Numbers were higher as word got out that these meetings were available. The meetings became an established part of the Spring Harvest programme. In 1992 about 300 people with mental handicaps attended the meetings provided for them. In 1993 a further week was added to the schedule by holding meetings at the Pwllheli venue as well.

This sort of development raised questions for A Cause for Concern. It made the managers realise that there were many people with mental handicaps needing spiritual help, and that most of them would never live in one of the charity's homes. What should be done for them? The question was before us at one of our prayer days, and our thoughts were focusing on the Gospel account of the feeding of the five thousand. As we pondered the question, Madeleine read some words from that account: 'They do not need to go away. You give them something to eat' (Mt 14:16). For us that was like direction from heaven! It was the beginning of Causeway.

Alongside of its caring work, the charity has developed Causeway as an initiative to encourage Christians and churches to respond to people with mental handicaps living with them in the community. Why wasn't this happening anyway? Two reasons recurred with almost monotonous regularity. First, people hadn't thought about the issue. It was not lack of concern but simple ignorance. Second, where people had some idea that there was an issue, they felt ill-equipped to respond.

Causeway's response to this was to produce three different resources. First, the *Christian Awareness Pack on Mental Handicap* addressed the ignorance. Second the *Do It Yourself Training Pack: The Local Church and Mental Handicap*, published in partnership with Scripture Union, enabled people to learn what they needed to know in order to do something practical. Third, *We're All Special To God* (also published by Scripture Union) was written to help those who were ready to set up and run Bible groups for people with mental handicaps.

Up to this point Causeway had been responding to increasing demand. Its resources and conferences were seeking to help people who knew they needed help. As a result several Bible groups were formed: in Haywards Heath and Harlow, in Bournemouth and Bedford—and elsewhere. In 1992 Causeway moved into a more proactive phase to encourage and assist the setting up of more groups. More resources have been produced to support this growing ministry—including music, tapes, training video and a simplified version of the Bible.

Let's pause for a moment. Our survey of past and present Christian involvement has revealed a generally disappointing picture of the level of concern. With some notable exceptions, it has shown the tendency of the church to reflect the attitudes of society.

It is disturbing also to observe that there appears to be a cycle in attitudes to the care of people with mental handicaps.

There was a surge of interested concern in the mid-eighteenth century which rapidly declined into tolerance of institutions like Bethlem. Again, in the mid-nineteenth century men like Andrew Reed were reversing the trend, but by the beginning of the twentieth century the march of Darwinism had padlocked the doors of the institutions against any hope of integration. The second half of the twentieth century has seemed to be a period of enlightenment so far as mental handicap is concerned. But as the 1990s advance, so compassion for people with mental handicaps seems to decline. Voices calling for their segregation again clamour for attention. The drive to close institutions in favour of ordinary housing is slowing down and other needs are taking precedence over the needs of people with mental handicaps.

What will the churches do this time? Will we follow the trend, having found the notion of integration too demanding, if we ever tried? Or will we act on what we believe and, by example and argument, ensure the recognition of people with mental handicaps as fully equal members of our communities and congregations?

There never were more opportunities for Christians to be involved in helping people with mental handicaps. The next chapter shows how legislation will now make local authorities more willing and able to use voluntary groups in meeting local needs. A Cause for Concern will be helping such groups, and Causeway is the first stage towards that as it encourages Christians to befriend people with mental handicaps, which may lead to providing help for them. Which may, in turn, lead to establishing residential care for them, bringing the story full circle.

Notes

[1] *UK Christian Handbook 1992/3* (Marc Europe: London, 1991), p 210.
[2] J. Mitchell-Innes, *The Church and the Care of Mentally Handicapped People in the Community* (Unpublished paper, 1992), p 22.

6

Who Cares?

All right! We accept that we haven't done as well as we ought in responding to people with mental handicaps. We admire what good Christian men and women have done, but you have to face the fact that there is more to this problem than the church can handle.

I think I know what's coming.

This isn't really our responsibility. The government ought to do what's needed. We are willing to help, but they are responsible.

Quite right too! At least to a certain extent.

The contribution Christians can make is limited and has to be made within the framework of government policy and legislation. So we need to know more about the context in which our response can be made. We will discover that we have wider opportunities than ever. But once again, we need to glance back in time to see how things have come to where they are.

The Dark Ages

The beginnings of institutional care, as we have already seen, grew out of a concern to provide training for people with mental handicaps. That was in the nineteenth century. As the twentieth century dawned it was apparent that the experiment had not been as successful as had been hoped. Other factors had come into play which were to lead to one of the most oppressive eras ever in the care of people with mental handicaps. The philosophy which gave birth to it has been called 'Social Darwinism'. The development which triggered it was the introduction of compulsory elementary education in the 1870s.[1]

Following legislation in England and Scotland, a system of elementary education was introduced based on literacy and numeracy. Children were tested by government inspectors, and teachers' pay was determined by the results of these tests. Consequently, children who were slow to learn were either excluded from education or placed in special classes. In the 1890s the Board of Education agreed that children who were 'feeble-minded' or 'mentally defective' should be segregated—a situation which has remained more or less the same for 100 years!

> Mental defect might have remained an 'educational problem' if the identification of defectives had not coincided with a moral panic about the quality of the population.[2]

In America Walter Fernald, a highly respected expert in the field of mental handicap, wrote for a National Conference in 1904:

> The modern American community is very intolerant of the presence of these dangerous defectives with the desires and passions of adult life, without control of reason or judgment. There is widespread and insistent demand that these women be put under control . . . the adult males become the town loafers and incapables, the irresponsible pests of the neighbourhood, petty thieves, purposeless destroyers of property, incendiaries, and very frequently violators of women and little girls.[3]

By this time Darwin's theory of evolution was widely believed and accepted as scientific. Its social dimension was taken to mean that, with increasing competition between the countries of Europe, the principle of the survival of the fittest required Britain to ensure the quality of its population.

The Boer War acted as a focus for the anxieties of the ruling elite . . . a large number of the conscripts had to be rejected as medically unfit. An interdepartmental committee was established on physical deterioration and when this reported in 1904 it tended to confirm the worst fears.[4]

Eugenics—improving the human race by 'selective breeding' —now became popular, supported by investigations claiming scientific respectability. Mental defect was 'proved' to be inherited and to be connected with crime, pauperism and prostitution.

By 1910 eugenics had become accepted both in the press and political debates. Not only was there a fear that mental defectives were extremely fertile, but there was a belief that they did not respond to normal moral constraints and tended to produce more offspring than other people. . . . A Royal Commission, which reported in 1908, accepted the eugenists' arguments that mental defect was a threat to society and that it was caused by the reproduction of existing defectives who tended to have more offspring than other people.[5]

To improve the quality of the population the upper classes were urged to have more children, and at the same time measures were introduced to prevent mental defectives from having children. The 1913 Mental Deficiency Act classified 'low-grade defectives' as imbeciles and idiots requiring care under the provisions of the Act.

Thus it was possible to organise the segregation of mental defectives from society at large, and within the institutions to further segregate the sexes. World War I impeded the progress of the Act, but the 1920s and 1930s saw a substantial increase in the number and size of institutions for people with mental handicaps. This period also saw the formation of the Wood Committee combining representatives of the

Board of Education and the Board of Control. Its report, published in 1929, stated:

> Families which have mentally defective members would include a much larger proportion of insane persons, epileptics, paupers, criminals (especially recidivists), unemployables, habitual slum dwellers, prostitutes, inebriates and other social inefficients. . . . This group comprises the lowest ten per cent in the social scale of most communities. . . . If we are to prevent the racial disaster of mental deficiency we must deal not merely with the mentally defective persons but with the whole sub-normal group from which the majority come. . . . The relative fertility of this group is greater than that of normal persons.[6]

How many of today's fears and prejudices can be traced back to this disastrous philosophy and legislation!

World War II dealt a significant blow to the credibility of Social Darwinism. The arrogance of Nazism and its 'superior race' mentality had left the awful scar of mass destruction of thousands of people whose only crimes were their disability or their Jewishness. The stirrings of a different view of mental deficiency was seen in a Royal Commission report in the 1950s and in a pamphlet by the National Council of Civil Liberties. However, change was a long time coming.

While tens of thousands lived (and died) in immense hospitals —many of which were, at some time, exposed for the scandalous and inhuman conditions tolerated—a novel notion began to percolate the thinking of professionals and legislators. Perhaps, after all, it was conceivable that the subnormal, as they became known, might actually be able to live in the community.

Two changes heralded this possibility. Once again changes in educational theory were having an impact. The 1971 Education Act set aside the assumption that 'the educationally subnormal' were ineducable. The training centres run by health authorities became special schools under the control of local education authorities. Parents were warned not to expect too much from the change, but as the years have passed standards and results improved.

A decade later the 1981 Education Act introduced a system by which all children with special educational needs could be identified and assessed. This Act also envisaged a significant degree of integration into mainstream education for people with mental handicaps. That integration has remained largely unrealised and special schools continue to be the main setting in which most children with mental handicaps receive their education.

The other major change, also in 1971, was the publication of the White Paper *Better Services for the Mentally Handicapped*. This found that very little had been done to develop services for people with mental handicaps in the community. It took seriously the fact that large numbers of people with mental handicaps were unnecessarily detained in institutions. It outlined ways in which they could move out into the community, setting targets for achievement by 1991. Those targets were not met. People already living in the community also needed services if they were not to be allowed access to the institutions. What was proposed required different organisational attitudes and staff with different skills. And there was, initially at least, considerable evidence of inertia on the part of authorities and institutions.

At about the same time a new view of mental handicap was spreading. Popularly known as 'normalisation', it was already well established in Scandinavia and America. Bengt Nirje, one of its originators, defined it as:

> making available to the mentally handicapped patterns and conditions of everyday life which are as close as possible to the norms and patterns of the mainstream of society.[7]

> Isolation and segregation nourish public ignorance and prejudice, while integration and normalisation of the ways of life of smaller groups of mentally retarded people provide the opportunities for the ordinary human relationships which are the basis for understanding and social acceptance and integration of the individual.[8]

If this could become the established attitude in society towards people with mental handicaps then they could expect the same opportunities for a meaningful and enjoyable life as any other citizen.

A number of developments in thinking were taking place in the various professions dealing with people with mental handicaps, and the introduction of the principle of normalisation seems to have been like a catalyst bringing together these new ideas into practical strategies. It has contributed greatly to the whole notion of community care by casting doubt on the value and rightness of traditionally segregated, hospital-based services for people with mental handicaps.

Wolf Wolfensberger, probably the most widely known proponent of normalisation, defined it as 'the utilisation of means which are as culturally normative as possible'. This does not mean we seek to make people with mental handicaps as 'normal' as possible. Rather it means that we will give them opportunities to live the sort of life that the rest of us regard as normal and ordinary. It poses the question: 'Why should a person be deprived of the experiences of everyday life we all value, on the grounds that he or she has a mental handicap?'

Most people can (and do) live in ordinary houses, eat ordinary food, travel on ordinary buses and shop in ordinary shops. Only some aspects of the lives of people with mental handicaps require special services, and even those services can usually be provided alongside those available to the general public.

Such a principle will significantly affect what is provided for people with mental handicaps, and has begun to do so to an increasing extent. Whereas they once received long-term care in hospitals in rural areas, they may now hope for a place in a more-or-less ordinary house in the community. (Please ignore the fire signs on the doors!) Such houses will be near bus routes and shops. They will be encouraged to spend their leisure time using community facilities, the library, swimming pool, theatre, church and pub. The principle also points to the desirability of ordinary jobs for people with mental handicaps—but they are less readily available at present.

The expression of the principle was primarily towards 'service provision'. John O'Brien took it further by seeking to focus on the individual with a mental handicap. He outlined 'five accomplishments' which have become a bench-mark for provision.

1 Community presence is the experience of sharing the ordinary places that define community life.

2 Choice is the experience of growing autonomy in both small, everyday matters and large, life-defining matters.

3 Competence is the experience of growing ability to perform skilfully functional and meaningful activities with whatever assistance is required.

4 Respect is the experience of having a valued place among a network of people and valued roles in community life.

5 Community participation is the experience of being part of a growing network of personal relationships which includes close friends.

The question to be answered by professionals is still, 'What services shall we provide?', but the starting point has changed. The service is a response to the person and his or her particular needs and aspirations. The process of deciding the shape of the service can be shared with the individual because a framework for involvement is provided. That is the ideal!

You will have seen some similarities between the principle of normalisation and the principle of personal value described in Chapter 2. The latter began from a different starting point and is entirely focused on the individual concerned. It too must be expressed in the way each of us relates to people with mental handicaps. And our failure to express such a principle in the past may explain why things are as they are.

From the 1970s onwards things have begun to happen— not spectacularly, not universally, not comprehensively, not quickly. But those who were involved as carers or 'pro- fessionals' at that time recognise that the situation which pertains today is vastly improved on that of twenty to thirty years ago. Some would add, with reason, 'Which goes to show how bad things were!'

The rising sun

During the 1980s there was a good deal more by way of
concerned debate about mental handicap than there had been
at any other time this century. The Committee of Enquiry
into Mental Handicap Nursing and Care (the Jay Committee)
published its report in 1979. It anticipated much of the debate
which was to follow by asking questions about how future
care would be provided, by whom, and with what training.
Much of what it proposed has been ignored, but the model
of care it outlined has set the standard for current provision.
It laid down five 'service principles':
1 Mentally handicapped people should use normal services
wherever possible.
2 Existing networks of community support should be
strengthened by professional services and not supplanted by
them.
3 Specialised services or organisations for mentally handicapped people should be provided only to the extent that
they can demonstrably meet or are likely to meet additional
needs that cannot be met by general services.
4 There should be a 'life plan' for every individual mentally
handicapped person so that co-ordination and continuity of
care may be achieved.
5 There should be someone to intercede on behalf of
mentally handicapped people to enable them to obtain
appropriate services.[9]

A year later the Kings Fund Centre published *An Ordinary
Life* which stimulated further the notion that people with
mental handicaps should be:

in the mainstream of life, living in ordinary houses in ordinary
streets, with the same range of choices as any citizen, and mixing
as equals with the other, and mostly not handicapped members
of their own community.[10]

In 1981 the government stated its clear support for the
principle of care in the community in a Department of Health

and Social Security document. In 1985 a follow-up document bemoaned the lack of progress.

The early 1980s also saw a change in the way people living in residential care homes were financed. One of the results was a substantial increase in the number of homes for dependent groups of people. Some people had seen in the new funding arrangements the opportunity to make a profit out of care, and not all the homes opened seemed too concerned about the type of care provided. Horror stories circulated of homes for elderly people where the only heating was by means of a mobile gas heater moved from one room to another! Registration procedures were minimal, costing only £1 initially and no further payments thereafter.

The Registered Homes Act (1984) came into force on 1st January 1985—and life has never been the same since for those in the independent sector. While the Act was broadly welcomed by charities in the mental handicap field, there was some resentment that its stringent demands did not apply to the local authorities own homes. Yet the local authorities were relatively free to develop and impose their own guidelines on others within the terms of the Act. This meant that very different standards could be found to apply in different counties. And it also resulted in much higher fees charged by the local authority on the proprietor—at initial registration, registration of the home manager (and his successors), plus an annual charge per bed space.

However, any organisation with a genuine concern for the people in its care could not fail to endorse the sentiments expressed in the Code of Practice published in connection with the Act:

Underlying all the recommendations and requirements set out in this Code is a conviction that those who live in residential care should do so with dignity; that they should have the respect of those who support them; should live with no reduction of their rights as citizens (except where the law so prescribes), and should be entitled to live as full and active a life as their physical and mental condition will allow.[11]

A government agency, the Audit Commission, stirred up any complacency which might have developed in Whitehall by publishing a critique of the care in the community policy. *Making a Reality of Community Care* appeared in 1986, being the result of a careful study of what was happening. It was by no means a pat on the back for government.

> There are serious grounds for concern about the lack of progress in shifting the balance of services towards community care . . . the community care policy is in danger of failing to achieve its potential. . . . Radical steps will be necessary if underlying problems are to be solved. Fine-tuning existing arrangements, or treating the symptoms will not meet the needs of the situation.[12]

This general picture was particularly true of services for people with mental handicaps compared with objectives set out in 1971. Furthermore, it seemed as though some people had been lost altogether!

> It must be a matter of grave concern that although there are 37,000 fewer mentally ill and mentally handicapped patients today than there were ten years ago, no one knows what has happened to many of those who have been discharged.[13]

Another report charged the government with 'wasting money and with allowing the private residential care sector to expand in a manner inimical to the development of care in the community'.[14]

Towards community care

Her Majesty's Stationery Office had a busy year in 1988, publishing two reports which related to residential care. The first to appear was an independent review of residential care chaired by Lady Wagner. Its message was summarised in its title: *Residential Care: A Positive Choice*. The committee was commissioned 'to review the role of residential care and the range of services given in statutory, voluntary and private residential establishments',[15] and to recommend changes. Essential to the report was the belief that:

People who move into a residential establishment should do so by positive choice, and living there should be a positive experience.[16]

The report argued convincingly that a wide range of forms of care should be available to those who could not cope with living independently—whether because of age, disability or mental handicap. Those who require care should be fully involved in deciding what level of help they require and in what type of setting it would be. 'People providing services should see themselves first and foremost as there to serve the interests of users.'[17] Pretty radical stuff.

The second report of 1988 came from a totally different quarter. Following the Audit Commission report the government appeared to dither as to what to do next. In the event it asked Sir Roy Griffiths to advise on how the changes required could be implemented to provide the level of service required within the resources available, which the commission said was possible.

Sir Roy is a businessman enjoying considerable success in the commercial sphere. In a relatively short time he produced a report which was succinct in its size but wide-ranging in its scope. But for Mrs Thatcher, the then prime minister, it had an unpalatable flavour—Sir Roy urged that local authorities should be given lead responsibility in community care, and the money needed to do the job.

Weeks slipped by, turning into months, until the first anniversary of the report's publication had come and gone. Her Majesty's government seemed reluctant to grasp the nettle. Eventually it came out in support of Sir Roy's proposals. The White Paper *Caring For People* was published late in 1989. It sold out in a few days! It became law in 1990 as part of the National Health Service and Community Care Act. Its full implementation took effect from April 1993. Without doubt, it sets out plans for the most wide-ranging change in provision for dependent people for many years. What is more, it offers to voluntary groups—which includes churches—the opportunity to play their part in responding to the needs of people around them. For this reason it is worth lingering over the White Paper.

> Community care means providing the services and support which people who are affected by problems of ageing, mental illness, mental handicap or physical or sensory disability need to be able to live as independently as possible in their own homes, or in 'homely' settings in the community. The Government is firmly committed to a policy of community care which enables such people to achieve their full potential.[18]

Thus the opening fanfare of the White Paper. It set out key objectives for 'service delivery'. (At this point you should be warned that the paper is heavy with jargon. It is a form of shorthand beloved of professionals but not too difficult to translate with a little imagination!)
— to promote the development of domiciliary, day and respite services to enable people to live in their own homes wherever feasible and sensible;
— to ensure that service providers make practical support for carers a high priority;
— to make proper assessment of need and good case management the cornerstone of high quality care;
— to promote the development of a flourishing independent sector alongside good quality public services;
— to clarify the responsibilities of agencies and so make it easier to hold them to account for their performance;
— to secure better value for taxpayers' money by introducing a new funding structure for social care.[19]
Achieving these objectives would require major changes in the way 'social care' had been provided. First, and most difficult for the government to accept, local authorities would be given lead responsibility. The distinction between health care and social care meant that continuing responsibility by the health authorities would be inappropriate. However,

local authorities were discouraged from 'empire building'. They were charged with planning services so as to make 'maximum use of the independent sector'. Voluntary organisations and private businesses would be encouraged to develop and provide services. What is more, government funding arrangements would ensure that it was in the interests of the local authorities to use the independent sector rather than to make their own provision.

The local authority must assess what the dependent persons need that they cannot provide for themselves—which could include mobility, personal care, domestic assistance, accommodation, etc—so as to decide whether services should be provided for them and in what form. This assessment is the key to all that will follow.

> The objective of the assessment is to determine the best available way to help the individual. Assessments should focus positively on what the individual can and cannot do, and could be expected to achieve, taking account of his or her personal and social relationships. . . . Assessments should take account of the wishes of the individual and his or her carer, and of the carer's ability to continue to provide care, and where possible should include their active participation. Effort should be made to offer feasible services which enable individuals and carers to make choices.[20]

Translating this into real-life situations may help to make clear what is intended. Mr and Mrs Bucknell's son, John, is forty-five years of age and severely mentally handicapped. Mr Bucknell has suffered a slight stroke which has left him paralysed in the right arm for the time being. He is no longer able to bath his son and, since he weighs 16 stone, Mrs Bucknell is certainly not able to take over this task. Prior to the Care in the Community legislation this scenario is capable of one solution—the time has obviously come for John to enter a residential care home. Although they know it is inevitable sooner or later, his parents are not keen on this as a solution.

Under the new legislation residential care will not be

offered as the first option since all John at present requires is some assistance with personal care. He can still live at home and still attend the Adult Training Centre during the day. The social services department case manager will assess the help required and will then contract with an agency able to provide a service (known as a service provider) which meets the need for personal care. It will obviously be much cheaper than paying the fee for full residential care and it will meet the need facing John and his family—a needs-led service, in the jargon.

> It will be the responsibility of the social services authority to design care arrangements in line with individual needs, in consultation with the client and other care professionals, and within available resources.[21]

The service will be kept under review to ensure that it continues to be appropriate to the need.

As the needs within the community are so diverse, the local authority is encouraged to ensure that the ways of meeting the needs are equally diverse. Here is another scenario, given me in conversation with a director of a social services department. Mrs Williams, aged seventy-nine years, is referred to the social services department by her doctor. She is a lonely widow who is finding it increasingly difficult to cook for herself. As a result she is depressed and underfed. The usual solution would be Meals on Wheels, which would solve the problem with cooking but would not address the problem of loneliness. The case manager assesses the need and makes an arrangement with the publican at the public house on the corner to provide Mrs Williams with a free meal three days a week, paid for by the department. Mrs Williams goes to the pub for lunch, meets other people from the locality, thus renewing or making friendships. She develops an informal network of local people who have become aware of her and are able to give her support. Both problems solved. It could, of course, be the local church which provides the meal and the company!

A clouded dawn?

The White Paper covers far more issues than are addressed here—you can buy your own copy if you want to know more—but enough has been said to give the flavour of what it proposes. People in the caring professions welcomed the emphasis on a 'needs-led service'. By beginning with people, the care provided can be tailored to their particular requirements, unlike the previous system which offered a limited and fixed response. But it has also resulted in a change of 'atmosphere' dominated by economics rather than care. Indeed one now hears reference to the 'care industry'!

One of the elements is the contractual relationship which it establishes. Strictly speaking contracts are not new, and those who have had their fingers burned for providing a service to a local authority which reneged on a 'gentlemen's agreement' will welcome something firm in writing. But the contract is between the local authority (the purchaser) and the organisation (the service provider). The individual for whom the service is obtained has no part in the contract— rather as my car has no part in the agreement I make with my garage about its repair! In some countries ways have been found to ensure that the voice of the individual is heard at this level.

Nor is it at present clear how long contracts will last. Where it relates to providing long-term residential care one hopes that the people concerned will be able to look on their new setting as home for as long as they wish. For a person with a mental handicap in, say, his thirties this will require more than a three-year contract if he is to feel any security in the arrangements. And if competitive tendering reveals that another independent organisation can provide the care more cheaply, will any regard be taken of the fact that he is settled where he is, thank you? As this happened before contracts were introduced one fears that it will be even more likely in the new climate.

Charities also face a challenge in finding ways to retain their independence in this new environment. They have been to the fore as advocates for people with mental handicaps and campaigners for better services. In future the structures they will want to change and the policies they will seek to influence will be those of their paymasters! Prudence may then suggest a more muted (and probably less effective) role as advocates.

Social services departments are having to adjust to very wide-ranging changes in structure to enable them to operate the new legislation. Staff have been retrained to enable them to fulfil the more financially sensitive roles they will have in future. Budgets have been dispersed so that they are managed by the people who will buy the new range of services. It is by no means clear what will happen if they run out of funds half-way through the year. Nor is it clear what they will do if they find themselves having to provide for more needy cases than those currently being funded. Whereas, at its dawn, the legislation promised that services would be deter-mined in terms of needs, as it reaches its zenith a different picture emerges—what can be achieved will be determined by the resources available.

Parents of children and adults with mental handicaps will not find this surprising. They know from experience that money is the bottom line. And they know that more is being spent on mental handicap services today than at any time before. Most districts now have a Community Mental Handi-cap Team (CMHT). A community nurse and a social worker form the core of the team, with access to a range of specialist services for people with mental handicaps. They provide a single door to services as varied as toy libraries and occupa-tional therapy, psychology and speech therapy. Advice is to hand on local facilities, national organisations and state benefits. Although the average family may not be aware of its existence, the National Development Team—established to advise on facilities for people with mental handicaps—has been vigorous in prodding local and health authorities to improve their services.

Having said all that, if you were to meet with almost any

group of parents of people with mental handicaps, you would find them discussing how far the services available fall short of their expectations and needs. Their commitment to caring for very dependent people does not blunt the readiness with which they will campaign for improvements for their offspring. At almost every meeting I have ever attended three main concerns are expressed—day services or employment, short-term care and long-term care for adults. That is not to say that children with mental handicaps do not present needs. Rather it reflects the fact that facilities for children are better, with help with early training and school places widely available from three years of age through to nineteen. There is also an acceptable level of short-term care up to sixteen years of age in most districts.

However, it is as childhood recedes that the demands of parenting increase and the support available diminishes. The new legislation does not offer much hope for change. Built into the plans for the future is the assumption that it is better for people to continue in their own home, and for adults with a mental handicap that home is in fact their parents'. This is not necessarily best for people with mental handicaps. Their development would benefit from the added stimulation of living apart from the family with people who will bring a different perspective on life for them.

The option is not one that is readily available. Crisis management has been the order of the day and looks set to continue. Even when homes in the voluntary sector have vacancies they frequently find that social services departments will not fund non-urgent placements. Yet, more than anything else, the parents of people with mental handicaps fear that the obvious long-term need for care will be resolved only when their situation becomes desperate. They realise that the transition from the family home to a residential care home will be traumatic for their son or daughter even in the best of circumstances. For that to take place in the face of family tragedy, serious illness or death renders the trauma unsupportable for individuals with a mental handicap. They will not only face a move to unfamiliar accommodation but also suffer the loss of a loved parent.

How much better to arrange the move at a time when the individual is emotionally able to cope, encouraging the development of a new sense of security before the inevitable death of parents and the end of the family home. A thorough research study was undertaken over a period of three years into the difficulties facing twenty families caring for young adults with severe learning difficulties. It found that three-quarters of the mothers lived in hope that their children would die before themselves. Some were determined to ensure this would happen rather than entrust their son or daughter to a system which had proved itself incapable of caring for him or her.[22]

Such desperation must provide a context in which one looks at what is happening as the new legislation comes into force and we become familiar with its way of working. In late 1991 the National Council for Voluntary Organisations warned: 'There is considerable concern that there will be increased demand for services alongside a static budget.'[23]

The same concern was repeated through 1992 and into 1993. A better-than-expected level of funding promised by the government is insufficient for the ambitious programme set out in community care plans.

This tends to encourage the cynical view that the assessment process will be a device for rationing demand rather than responding to it! The more so since there is no legal requirement of the local authority to meet the needs it identifies.

Another trend which appears in some community care plans is that services for people with mental handicaps will be reduced from present levels. One county council plan put it like this:

The care social services can offer must be targeted to people in greatest need and this means difficult decisions have to be made about *priorities between groups* of clients as well as between individuals.

Over past years social services has allocated a large share of new resources to services for people with mental handicaps—now emphasis is shifting to people who are elderly and to children and families.[24]

All of this is taking place against the background of discovering that care in the community is actually more expensive than institutional care. Authorities are backing away from their earlier idealism. Where once they were insisting that 'small is beautiful', now 'larger is economical'. Some hospital closure plans have been slowed down.

With so much still to be done, with authorities less and less able to respond, and with a legislative framework within which to work, there is opportunity for churches to get involved in supporting and providing social care as never before this century. The fact is that many of the services which will be required do not at present exist within the voluntary sector. Businesses will not provide them because they will be uneconomic. But churches have premises which stand idle for much of the time. They have people who are motivated by the love of God, whose interest is not in profit but in bringing relief and hope into the lives of needy people in their community.

The new climate may produce some concerns but it also provides opportunities. It would be a sad comment on our vision if Christians, of all people, failed to respond to the opportunity to take again their place as leaders and innovators in shaping a caring community for people with needs.

Notes

[1] I am indebted to Andy Alaszewski's 'From villains to victims' in A. Leighton (ed), *Mental Handicap in the Community* (Woodhead-Faulkner: Cambridge, 1988), pp 3–13.

[2] *Ibid*, p 4.

[3] W. Fernald, quoted by R. Edgerton, *Mental Retardation* (Fontana: London, 1979), p 107.

[4] Alaszewski, *op cit*, p 5.

[5] *Ibid*.

[6] Quoted by T. Stainton, 'A Terrible Disaster to the Race', *Community Living* (January 1992): p 18.

[7] Quoted in Leighton, *op cit*, p 102.

[8] *Ibid*, p 112.

[9] O. Russell, in M. Craft, J. Bicknell, S. Hollins (eds), *Mental Handicap* (Balliere Tindall: London, 1985), p 10.

[10] Quoted by D. Towell, *ibid*, p 16.

[11] *Home Life* (Centre for Policy on Ageing: UK, 1984), p 15.

[12] Audit Commission, *Making a Reality of Community Care* (HMSO: London, 1986), p 13.

[13] *Ibid*, p 17.

[14] G. Wagner, *A Positive Choice* (HMSO: London, 1988), p 1.

[15] *Ibid*, p 1.

[16] *Ibid*, p 7.

[17] *Ibid*, p 12.

[18] *Caring for People* (HMSO: London, 1989), p 3.

[19] *Ibid*, p 5.

[20] *Ibid*, pp 18–19.

[21] *Ibid*, p 21.

[22] J. Hubert, *Home-bound* (King's Fund Centre: UK, 1991).

[23] 'The Mixed Economy of Care', *Community Care Information Service: Newsletter no 3* (Winter 1991/2): p 1.

[24] *Caring for People in Berkshire; Community Care Plan 1992/3* (Berkshire County Council, April 1992), p 3.

7
Why Should I Care?

Christians have a double dilemma concerning mental handi-cap. Like the rest of society they have a struggle with differentness and the fear which it generates. Unlike the rest of society they have a struggle of faith when confronted with something which does not fit comfortably with their preferred way of seeing the world. It is not surprising, therefore, if many find themselves better able to cope by 'passing by on the other side'. It is not malice aforethought, nor even lack of compassion. It is more an expression of helplessness, of not knowing what to do or how best to respond. The fact that it is understandable—and which of us has not employed this tactic at one time or another—ought not to make it acceptable. We must learn to face issues which seem to us difficult if we are to grow in faith and understanding. This chapter aims to help that process forward.

Jesus made it clear that, so far as God is concerned, our motivation is at least as important as our actions. It is relatively easy to feel pressurised into helping people with mental handicaps by the outstanding example of non-Christians. 'If they are doing something, so should we.' Their example is a challenge. If they were to withdraw from the scene, most of the charitable work undertaken for people with mental handicaps would simply cease to exist! There is an even higher challenge to us than that example. It is the challenge of what God expects from those who say that they love him. It is the challenge to work out in real life the requirements God sets before us in the Bible. Our task is to relate those requirements to the real life situation we are considering. That will help us to know what we should do and will provide some insights as to how we should do it. Most importantly, it will show why we should be active in our response.

Mental handicap confronts three major theological questions. It raises 'the problem of suffering' and the related issue of healing, particularly for people with mental handicaps. It requires us to consider what place 'social concern' has as a Christian duty, and challenges us to look at the 'spiritual versus secular' divide. It confronts contemporary priorities by drawing us towards the seeming upside-downness of biblical attitudes.

The problem of suffering

We may already be begging the question by implying that mental handicap is acceptable and unavoidable. Where does it fit with our understanding that God is love? Should we not be praying for the healing of people with mental handicaps? We can only answer these questions by considering the wider issue of suffering in the world. In a few pages we cannot hope to solve the problem or to consider fully the dilemmas which are presented. Nor can we side-step the challenge altogether.

John stood at the front door waiting for an answer to his knock. He was visiting on behalf of his church in a street which stood in the shadow of a large children's hospital. One half of the hospital was medical; the other provided long-term care for children with mental handicaps, some of whom were very severely handicapped. At last the householder opened the door and John explained his mission. The man nodded in the direction of the hospital, 'How can you expect me to believe in a God who allows things like that?' There was a pause before John answered. 'My son lives there,' he said.

It has been my case all along that mental handicap is not something 'wrong'. That is not to say that its occurrence does not involve suffering. There is the pain of disappointment for parents who feel cheated by the birth of a baby with a handicap. There will be prolonged and more demanding parenting. There will be the discomfort of visiting clinics where the other babies are bouncing with health and brimming with development. There will be the awkwardness of friends towards what has happened. There will be the seemingly endless tussle with authorities to get the best for the child. There is the struggle with life that the more severely handicapped child has. There may be more frequent illness, more hospitalisation, more surgery. There will be a struggle for acceptance facing the mildly mentally handicapped person. There will be the hurt of rejection, the anguish of discrimination. There will be the feeling of 'not-right-ness' surrounding the whole experience. First the parent, and later maybe the child, will wrestle with the questions: 'Why?' 'Why me?' 'Why us?' All of which is part of the dilemma facing the thoughtful Christian: Why does God allow it to happen like this?

Our response to this requires a fixed point for our compass. It is this: God is good! The cynic may goad us with the question, 'If God is a God of love . . .? How can a good God allow . . .?' We cannot yield him the ground he claims. Though his protest is popular, the cynic betrays a common failing. C.S. Lewis put it like this:

> We want, in fact, not so much a Father in Heaven as a grandfather in heaven. . . . Love is something more stern and splendid than mere kindness.[1]

He developed the theme further:

> When Christianity says that God loves man, it means that God loves man: not that he has some 'disinterested', because really indifferent, concern for our welfare, but that, in awful and surprising truth, we are the object of his love. You asked for a

loving God: you have one. The great spirit you so lightly invoked, the 'lord of terrible aspect', is present: not a senile benevolence that drowsily wishes you to be happy in your own way, not the cold philanthropy of a conscientious magistrate, nor the care of a host who feels responsible for the comfort of his guests, but the consuming fire himself, the Love that made the worlds, persistent as the artist's love for his work and despotic as a man's love for a dog, provident and venerable as a father's love for a child, jealous, inexorable, exacting as love between the sexes. How this should be, I do not know: it passes reason to explain why any creatures, not to say creatures such as we, should have a value so prodigious in their Creator's eyes.[2]

If God is not good, then he must be indescribably evil. If God is not just then the devil must seem merciful. There are no alternatives. We claim that God is God and by that mean that he has power to control the world and what happens in it. We cannot then exempt this or that aspect of life which does not seem 'nice' and say that God has nothing to do with it or that he can't do anything about it. Either we accept what the Bible says when it speaks of the goodness and justice of God, or we had best admit to being unbelievers and abandon what will be to us a religious charade. No other options are open to us.

Is it, then, reasonable to hold on to our faith? Yes, indeed it is. It is not mindless believism which convinces us of the goodness of God. There is so much within our experience of the world about us that demonstrates the goodness of God. The sheer beauty and variety of what we see is evidence that God cares deeply. There is so much in our experience of life which further confirms that God loves us. We must set over against the negative and hurtful trials and testings, the too-many-to-number blessings and pleasures which we enjoy. How many times in how many different ways our days have come to life with some unsought and unexpected delight.

Supremely, our confidence in the goodness of God is based upon the Bible, which is God's revelation to us of how things really function. It gives us the desperately needed insight into what is going on in the world about us.

> To the Bible God's power and goodness are both axiomatic. God is love. The whole Bible story is the story of that goodness and love. . . . God made a good world and he made man as the crown of his creation. Man was made for fellowship with God, to love him person to Person. Man misused his powers of understanding and his powers of choice and was thrust from Paradise.[3]

It is this 'saving love' which is, without question, the greatest demonstration that God is love.

> No Christian dare doubt God's goodness in permitting the most grievous suffering, when he remembers the means God chose for the overthrow of evil. It was in the depth of human agony that Christ 'bore our sins in his body on the tree'. Not only tortured in body and forsaken by his friend, but cut off from his Father and become 'a curse for us', he suffered what no other man has suffered. . . . What a source of strength to know that he does not ask of us more than he was prepared himself to give.[4]

The second thing one has to say about suffering is, 'That's the way it is!' No matter how undesirable and distasteful it is to us, we cannot expect a problem-free existence. Life is not like that! Whether it be catastrophe, or just the slow grind of nagging pain, life and suffering are, for the time being, inextricably interwoven. This is not fatalism but realism.

To state things as baldly as this might suggest that there is a problem with the design, with the way we and the world are made. That is not the case. Rather it is because the design has been violated wilfully. All human suffering stems from the fact that the world has been devastated by sin. Our forebears set the process in motion by disobeying the only rule God gave them. Thereafter every human being who has ever lived—with only one exception—has carried forward the awful effects, so much so that the creation itself groans under the results (see Romans 8:22–23).

Some would want to extend this biblical teaching beyond the Bible. They will argue that suffering must originate from some particular misdemeanour. They resurrect the fable that the birth of a handicapped person is somehow a judgement from God on the parents. This is far from being the case. Rather it is symptomatic of the wider malaise which affects the universe!

Even so we have to acknowledge that human actions can have awful consequences. Immorality brings a dreadful toll on the promiscuous person. Drunken drivers bring terrible tragedy on others. Careless industrialists pollute the environment with lethal chemicals. Some forms of mental handicap are due to lead poisoning, and some to drugs and vaccines. Some can be blamed on incompetence by physicians. We bear some of the responsibility for our dilemma.

Although suffering is something we all want to avoid it is also something from which we can benefit. We may respond with bitterness which eats at the vitals of our being. Or we may let it work positively to make better people of us. The way we respond is crucial. Mental handicap has broken many marriages. It has also cemented others. It has brought devastation and despair. It has also inspired outstanding compassion and philanthropy.

What about healing and mental handicap? Almost every time I speak about mental handicap to groups of Christians I am asked about healing. (Except, on reflection, in theological colleges. They probably have the answer sorted out already!) Why not pray for mentally handicapped people to be healed?

My first response to this is to challenge the underlying assumption that there is something wrong, that somehow mental handicap is to be eliminated, that our concept of average intelligence matches God's. My second response is that if they are ill then, by all means, pray for their healing. Mental handicap is not in itself an illness. There is no antibiotic to cure it, no therapy to remove it. So healing is not what is required. That is not to suggest that prayer will not be of value to the person with a mental handicap. I know individuals who have been healed from various disorders related to their mental handicap. I have known situations where a person with a mental handicap has been 'prayed through' difficulties which were causing distress or disruptive behaviour. I know individuals who have learned to cope with their handicap in new ways following their conversion. I know a man with mental handicap who has been healed from cancer. But in every instance known to me, the person still has a mental handicap.

An enormous amount of damage has been done by well-meaning Christians praying over a mentally handicapped person for healing from his or her handicap. Profound disappointment has followed when there was no improvement in intellectual ability. The embarrassment and sense of failure for the person with a mental handicap has been real and traumatic.

Over the years I have met many parents who are praying for the healing of their mentally handicapped son or daughter. Some speak of improvements they have seen, which is tremendous. But, in spite of knowing scores, perhaps hundreds of people with mental handicaps, I have not yet heard a first-hand report of a person being changed from having a mental handicap to not having a mental handicap due to a sudden, supernatural intervention. I have no doubt that such an intervention is possible—after all, God is God!

But, perhaps, the fact that 'healing' is not given tells us something about how God sees mental handicap. It may also tell us something about suffering.

Social concern

Several years ago I was asked to speak at a regional assembly of a group of churches. The pattern was common at the time: afternoon meeting, tea, evening rally. I was billed to address both. In the afternoon I described how God intended that Christians should be 'a people that are his very own, eager to do what is good' (Tit 2:14). In conversations at teatime many expressed warm appreciation for the afternoon ministry. However, at the outset of the evening meeting the chairman told the congregation that several people had expressed to the organising committee their concern about the earlier session. So the committee wished to reaffirm their belief that salvation is by faith alone and not the result of our good works. The chairman then quoted from Ephesians 2:8–9.

I was hopping mad! The discourtesy was bad enough. The misuse of Scripture was even worse because it was so selective. Had he also read the following sentence in Ephesians 2, the chairman would have been more cautious about his statement:

> (Eph 2:8) For it is by grace you have been saved, through faith— and this not from yourselves, it is the gift of God—(9) not by works, so that no-one can boast. (10) For we are God's workman- ship, created in Christ Jesus to do good works, which God prepared in advance for us to do.

Fifteen to twenty years ago such an attitude was common among British evangelicals. Seeing the social dimension of living biblically is a relatively recent return to a more traditional stance. As John Stott writes:

> It is exceedingly strange that any followers of Jesus Christ should ever have needed to ask whether social involvement was their concern, and that controversy should have blown up over the relationship between evangelism and social responsibility.[5]

A glimpse at church history shows that Christians have played an influential part in civilising the human race! Not that the twentieth century can claim to be free of brutality with its record of horrendous wars and arsenals of sophisticated weapons of mass destruction. But generally speaking, every- day life in the Western world is immeasurably more humane than it was for ordinary people in the historic civilisations of the ancient world in Egypt, Babylon, Greece and Rome. The major factor in this humanising process has undoubtedly been the impact of Christian compassion.

> Social action in mission can be traced from the time of the apostles. . . . Concern was never limited to relief. The itinerating missionary carried with him a bag of medicines, new or better seed and plants, and improved livestock. Nevins introduced the modern orchard industry into Shantung. The Basel missionaries revolutionised the economy of Ghana by introducing coffee and cocoa grown by families and individuals on their own lands. James McKean transformed the life of Northern Thailand by eliminating its three major curses—smallpox, malaria, and leprosy. . . . The missionaries were constantly the protectors of the native peoples against exploitation and injustice by government and commercial companies.[6]

These are but a few examples which could be multiplied almost endlessly.

British history rings with the familiar names of Christians who are remembered for their contribution to the well-being of the nation or their outstanding example in charitable activities. Chief among them are William Wilberforce and Lord Shaftesbury. The political activities of these two men transformed the lives of slaves, lunatics, children in mines and women in mills. It was an evangelical Christian, Dr T.R. Armitage, who introduced and promoted the use of Braille— the first book to be embossed was the Bible. John Wesley, Dr Barnardo, Charles Haddon Spurgeon and George Muller did so much to ease the plight of unwanted and orphaned children. John Groom's work for people with physical dis-abilities, Agnes Weston and Elsie Sandes' concern for servicemen, E.J. Mather's mission to deep-sea fishermen— and more than can be listed here—all illustrate the concern of Christians to improve the lot of the disadvantaged and marginalised. It is not too much to claim that a great deal of the social work of the twentieth century has its roots in Christian charitable activity in the nineteenth.

If this concern has been such a part of Christian witness

for so long, what was it that turned so many away from social involvement—and still makes some reluctant to recognise a responsibility in this respect?

To understand this we need to go back to the beginning of this century. Theological liberalism was extending its deadening influence. It argued for a 'social gospel' which proposed that Christians could bring in the kingdom of God on earth by a process of social reconstruction. Change the environment and people will change—that was the underlying idea. It made it unnecessary to preach an outdated message of forgiveness through faith in Christ and diminished the importance of his death as a sacrifice for sins.

Christians who were trying to preach and live by the Bible fought shy of this emphasis—and anything which might appear to suggest approval of it! They became preoccupied with restating and defending the essential truths of the gospel, finding themselves with little time or inclination to consider social issues. And then came two world wars, bringing devastating disillusion in their wake. Changing people through social action seemed more than ever irrelevant. Human depravity looked incorrigible.

There was another strand of Christian thought which militated against concern for social issues—the doctrine of the Second Coming of Christ. Premillennialism was widespread. This particular interpretation of the New Testament teaches that the world will get worse as the Saviour's Second Advent draws nearer. This seemed to be borne out by the events of the time, and there was little point trying to reform society if it was shortly to be eclipsed. And by this time evangelical Christians were so identified with the middle classes that they were somewhat remote from the pressure of social need anyway!

By a strange double-think, social concern was acceptable in Christian missionary work. There was no hesitation in sending Christians to Third World countries to dig wells, to teach agriculture, to set up and run schools and, especially, to provide medical care. But even this worthy work was not without its embarrassment. Missionaries on furlough found themselves having to validate their caring ministry by emphasising to home congregations that they ran ward services in their hospitals, preached the gospel before dispensing medicine in their clinics and taught parables when they handed out seeds and harvested crops.

Just as a growing awareness of social responsibility was beginning to dawn again on British Christians, the charismatic movement burst upon the scene. Its particular form of spirituality, its sometimes divisive vitality, its different centre of gravity, created a preoccupation with structures and church life. Preventing or healing division became primary concerns in traditional churches. Finding new patterns of church life and relationship between congregations became the foci for burgeoning house churches. Social concern was well down the list of priorities.

Thankfully, as the twentieth century draws to a close, there is renewed social awareness and concern. It must find its biblical roots if it is to meet the tremendous challenges and opportunities which will face Christians as the year 2000 romps towards us.

Anyone who reads the Bible with an open mind must be moved by the concern God shows for human need. It is not a matter of quoting a text from Leviticus and another from the Sermon on the Mount, with perhaps an odd remark from one of Paul's letters thrown in. It crops us everywhere you look—whether in legislation, songs of praise, historical narrative, prophetic statements or wherever. And not only in the texts but in the very truths the Bible teaches as well. John Stott makes the point tellingly:

Why should Christians get involved in the world and its social problems? In reply, I propose to marshal five great doctrines of the Bible, which all of us already believe in theory, but which we tend to cut and trim in order to make them fit our escapist theology. My plea is that we have the courage to hold these doctrines in their biblical fullness. Any one of them should be sufficient to convince us of our Christian social responsibility; the five together leave us without excuse.[7]

The five doctrines he then deals with in some detail are these:

1 A fuller doctrine of God which recognises his position as God of nature, not just religion; as God of creation, not just his people; as concerned with justice, as well as justification.

2 A fuller doctrine of man as being made in God's likeness and therefore deserving of respect and compassion.

3 A fuller doctrine of Christ as Son of Man and Son of God who came in response to human need.

4 A fuller doctrine of salvation which accepts the rule of God and the lordship of Christ, working out both in faith and love.

5 A fuller doctrine of the church which accepts its role as witness to the world and a sanctifying, improving influence in it.

There isn't much left which does not speak to our duty of social concern and engagement!

A purpose for living

One of the tremendous by-products of becoming a Christian is to discover that life is both meaningful and purposeful. I am not just the result of chance events. I am here for a reason. What makes for an even greater sense of wonder is that God is involved in this as well. I am part of what he is doing in the world. I am here for his sake as well as my own. A non-Christian must find this almost impossible to believe and would understandably accuse me of being unforgivably pompous! But it really is true.

I have already quoted Ephesians 2:10 but it bears repetition:

> For we are God's workmanship, created in Christ Jesus to do good works, which God prepared in advance for us to do.

The Christians in Ephesus, to whom Paul first wrote these words, were well used to his teaching. The apostle had spent more than two years in this important city of the Roman Empire. For much of that time he had taught and debated daily in a lecture hall. Those who were converted would have known the excitement of his soaring theology, reflected in this letter which he later wrote to them from imprisonment in Rome.

The opening section of his letter presents a breathtaking view of the eternal God working purposefully in the arena of human history. His activity touches the lives of ordinary people who 'hope in Christ', drawing them into a powerful strategy which embraces the raising of Jesus from the clutches of death to establish him 'far above all' so that he 'fills everything in every way'.

Almost without a pause Paul rushes on to draw in finer detail the involvement of each Christian in this ongoing picture. In spite of their complete unsuitability, because spiritually dead, God has brought them to life too so that they can share with God's Son in time the prospect, and in eternity the reality, of heaven. Now, he says, this is something God has achieved in you. You deserved nothing and have been given everything—you have nothing to boast about. God has made us what we are so that we can do what he has already prepared for us to do: good works. What a theology for mere humans!

God wants us to do good. He has given us the potential. He has made it possible. And there is no shortage of good to be done.

There is a similar idea in the letter Paul wrote to Titus:

. . . our great God and Saviour, Jesus Christ . . . gave himself for us to redeem us from all wickedness and to purify for himself a people that are his very own, eager to do what is good' (Tit 2:13–14).

This is a quite different letter from Paul's letter to Ephesian Christians. It is written to a friend who is acting pastor in a church Paul had founded in Crete. The congregation there seems to have been apathetic and argumentative. Advising a young pastor in such circumstances is one thing. Inspiring him is another, especially when there are issues to be resolved about church structure and leadership.

The apostle's method is to point Titus to the wider spiritual context of his ministry—God's strategic purpose in the world. He writes about the 'blessed hope of the glorious appearing of our great God and Saviour, Jesus Christ' (2:13). The future consummation of history is in his sights as he describes what God has done to prepare for this and how we are involved in that preparation. We have been bought out of helplessness to be God's own people who are 'eager to do what is good' (2:14).

'Teach this, Titus,' Paul seems to say. 'Counteract their apathy with this perspective.' Later in the letter he warns against getting bogged down in theological arguments:

> Those who have trusted in God, [must] be careful to devote themselves to doing what is good. These things are excellent and profitable for everyone. (Tit 3:8).

The importance of these two passages is that they give us an insight into what God has in mind for his world and for us. He wants us to do something good for the world in which he has put us.

It's high time we asked what the Bible means by 'good works'. It offers no definition, which at first sight is a little disappointing. However, it is likely that some, at least, of what would have been listed in, say, AD 50, would no longer be relevant to us. Suppose it identified the care of people with leprosy—how would we now respond to that in Britain, other than at arms length? Suppose it specified protection for travellers—as on the road from Jerusalem to Jericho— our doing good would by now be institutionalised in professional protection agencies (or an angelic Securicor?). By leaving the definition open it enables us to make both a universal and a personal application which is relevant to the age, needs and place in which we find ourselves.

There are two obvious points to make. First, this is a matter requiring effort. The Bible speaks of works rather than pleasures. They are something we do. Second, these works are good. That suggests that the motivation is wholesome, the methods acceptable and the effects beneficial. They are to be consistent with the standards and intentions of the God who intends that we do them and inspires the doing.

We can develop our understanding of good works further by looking at the life and ministry of Jesus. The apostle Peter summarised it for Cornelius and his friends like this: 'He went around doing good and healing all who were under the power of the devil' (Acts 10:38). That fits with the robust testimony of the Gospel writers. Whether you read Mark or John, Matthew or Luke, you take the strong impression that Jesus was an influence for good wherever he went. Imagine the hope that must have grown in the hearts of people with leprosy when they heard that this man would touch them and could heal them. Notice how children were at ease in his company, and how protective mothers brought their infants to him for blessing. Where Jesus went greed was turned into generosity, animosity into acceptance. The records show him as thoughtful and helpful, sensitive and caring, gentle but strong, perceptive but unthreatening—especially to those who were weak. In fact 'goodness' expresses well the life that he lived.

Notice, too, that the life of Jesus was geared towards people. He was not preoccupied with philosophy, though the world-view he espoused has had a more profound influence than any other school of thought before or since. His priority was not to correct bad theology or to teach a new system of doctrine, though his revelation of truth was more far-reaching than anything man has otherwise received. He came, the Son of God as Son of Man, to serve his Father by serving people. His life was among them. He taught those who were his companions. He preached to crowds. He put his arm around distraught fathers and touched social outcasts. He comforted bereaved women. Here was God in touch with people.

Jesus intended that his life should be the example we need in respect of good works. 'This is to my Father's glory, that you bear much fruit, showing yourselves to be my disciples' (Jn 15:8). 'As the Father has sent me, I am sending you' (Jn 20:21). This is God's good purpose for the Christian's life.

So now we know what is expected of us. In what manner are we to fulfil God's expectations?

Love is the way it's done

Matthew reported a conversation between Jesus and a lawyer. (An 'expert in the law' was one versed in Jewish religious law and was usually a Pharisee.) The legal profession of the day was intensely interested in putting God's commands in some sort of priority order. Given their particular approach to religious life, that it was to do with keeping rules, it was an understandable issue to debate. More than once Jesus responded to them in much the same way.

> One of them, an expert in the law, tested him with this question: 'Teacher, which is the greatest commandment in the Law?' Jesus replied: 'Love the Lord your God with all your heart and with all your soul and with all your mind.' This is the first and greatest commandment. And the second is like it: 'Love your neighbour as yourself.' All the Law and the Prophets hang on these two commandments.' (Mt 22:35–40).

The fact that we are so familiar with this account obscures for us how revolutionary it was.

When you try to trace what part of the Old Testament Jesus was quoting from you stumble on an interesting fact. The first command is simple enough—it was spoken by Moses during his final sermon to the people of Israel as they were on the verge of entering the Promised Land. It seemed to be his way of summarising God's requirements of his people (Deut 6:4–6). Love for God is of primary importance.

Nothing precedes that, and all our obedience of his commands is seen as an expression of the relationship. Servile, mindless subjugation to a tyrannical deity is not part of biblical religion.

The second command Jesus mentions—Love your neighbour as yourself—similarly describes a relationship. It will secure respect for another person's property, family and reputation as required in the Ten Commandments. But Moses didn't make it part of his valedictory statement. What, then, is Jesus quoting from when he answers the lawyer? This commandment is found in an obscure passage in Leviticus, among a long list of prohibitions: 'Do not seek revenge or bear a grudge against one of your people, but love your neighbour as yourself. I am the Lord' (Lev 19:18). It may be that the lawyers had also found this statement and begun to recognise its significance, or that they learned about it from Jesus. (On another occasion a lawyer quoted it to Jesus—see Luke 10:27.) What must have shaken them rigid was what Jesus went on to say—that everything else hung on these two commands. The word picture he used is of a peg or nail driven into a wall on which other things are hung. In other words, the law could not be understood apart from these two commands; the prophets do not make sense apart from these two commands.

We have hit on something of tremendous importance. This is the key to living in a way that will please God and gain his approval. Love God; love your neighbour. It's all summed up in those two things. Or, as Paul puts it: 'Be imitators of God . . . live a life of love' (Eph 5:1–2). Which also explains why this is so important. It's the way God lives!

For simplicity it would be hard to better this, but it is exceptionally demanding in practice. You don't need to be a lawyer to see that, and one lawyer who did see it immediately realised that he was cornered, even condemned, by what he knew. 'He wanted to justify himself, so he asked Jesus, "And who is my neighbour?"' (Lk 10:29). That is the key question to which we must now find the answer, especially if we are expected to love them as we love ourselves.

In giving his reply Jesus told one of his most famous parables—the story of the Good Samaritan. A traveller on the road from Jerusalem to Jericho was attacked by bandits, robbed and left for dead. A timid priest saw him lying in the road but scuttled guiltily on his way. A proud Levite crossed over to avoid the embarrassment of seeing his sorry state. An alien—different in race and religion—took pity on the traveller and, at risk to his own safety, spent time tending his wounds before moving him to a place of safety. He paid for the man's keep until he was well enough to travel again. Then Jesus came back to the question by posing his own:

'Which of these three do you think was neighbour to the man who fell into the hands of robbers?' The expert in the law replied, 'The one who had mercy on him.' Jesus told him, 'Go and do likewise' (Lk 10:36–37).

The story tells who to love, who our neighbour is. The person to be loved is the person in need of love! Our word 'neighbour' suggests to us someone with whom we may have a lot in common. Our neighbour lives in the same street, is probably of similar social standing and race. Not so in this instance. The two men were on different sides of racial animosity that stretched back centuries. But the Samaritan had the means of meeting the needs of the Jewish traveller. That's the key—need and the power to meet need creates neighbour obligations. Hold on to that for a moment.

The story tells us also how to love. The sentimental aspect is ignored. This is compassion, a real and practical concern for the other person. Perhaps the priest and the Levite felt sympathy, but the Samaritan was moved to action. He did what he could, using what he had, to bring help in the way it was needed. And he did it for someone who at the time was incapable of rewarding or repaying him. He was loving his neighbour as himself; doing for him what he would want done in similar circumstances.

Now let's apply this to the issue of mental handicap. There

is no question that people with mental handicaps have needs and that to some of those needs we are able to respond. They will vary from person to person and may include physical, intellectual, emotional, social and spiritual needs. At some level every one of us can make a contribution, can express love. It may be by giving friendship or teaching someone how to bake a cake; by praying together, or providing employment. But the motivation is not to be, 'I suppose I ought to do something.' It is to be out of a practical, thoughtful response to the person, an expression of love.

This command to love has, as we have seen, a crucial place in Christian living which pleases God. It is the very 'social concern' which we may have thought of as peripheral to our lives. And it is curious to wonder why God considers it so important. Perhaps it is because he wants to ensure that human needs are met. Perhaps it is because he wants people to feel loved in a tangible way. Perhaps it is both. If it is either, there are lots of people out there in the world who are still waiting to experience what God wants us to provide!

And this is how it's done

Perhaps, unwittingly, the decline in social concern among Christians already referred to has something to do with the daunting responsibility it places upon us. Already, the idea that we are obliged to love people on the basis of negative qualities—needs—rather than those which are attractive may prove awesome. It is time to look at resources.

God has committed himself to 'meet all your needs according to his glorious riches in Christ Jesus' (Phil 4:19). That includes the power to love, indeed the result of his Spirit living in us is, first and foremost, love. So when he commands us firmly to love our neighbour it is not heartlessly done. He ensures that the power to do this is available to us in response to faith.

I have never been able to follow the 'let go and let God' view of faith. Nor does it seem to me that faith can be understood as 'a leap in the dark'. The first is too passive, too inactive to bear the sense the Bible wants to convey. The second is too chancy, too irrational.

'Faith' is a word we use in a variety of ways. We speak of our beliefs as our faith, when we mean something like a system of doctrines. We speak of our trust in God as faith too, when we mean our dependence on him for life, salvation and daily help. Both are right of course, expressing different aspects of what faith means. We could express the relationship between the two as a formula: Belief + Trust = Faith. Belief is the system of truths on which our faith stands. Trust is active dependence arising from what we believe.

Abraham is the Bible's chief example of faith. As Abram, he was told by God to leave the civilisation of Ur of the Chaldees and go to a place to which God would lead him. It must have been quite a wrench to take up the life of a nomad, having lived with street lighting and indoor bathrooms —thousands of years before Christ! But Abram believed what God said to him. And he trusted God to keep his part of the agreement by leading him and providing for him and his family—which God did!

A person becomes a Christian by faith. He believes what God has said about wrong and sin in his own life, and about Jesus' death for his sin. He trusts in Jesus to forgive him and make him a child of God. The New Testament is clear that we cannot earn forgiveness by doing good, as if our goodness was equal to the effect of Jesus' death! It is equally clear that those who through faith have become Christians will, by that same faith, live as Christians. That will involve them in being good and doing good. It will also mark them out as Christians. Jesus put it like this: 'By their fruit you will recognise them' (Mt 7:20). So it will not be a surprise if a Christian is more holy, more religious, or more evangelistic. Christians should also be more compassionate, more responsive to human need, more willing to do something about human need.

At this point depression may be setting in for some readers! 'Not again,' you say. 'Not someone else laying yet another burden on my back, wringing the last drop of energy from my weary spirit.' Not at all! The whole point of Pentecost was the giving of the Holy Spirit so that we could do by God's power in us what was simply beyond us on our own. And the Spirit is activated in us through faith. It really is that simple and uncomplicated.

James, the brother of Jesus, was convinced that genuine religion must be practical. And he showed how it can be—through the exercise of faith. In his letter in the New Testament he envisaged a situation which he must have seen in his church, and which has been repeated endlessly down the centuries. A visitor comes into the service and is obviously destitute. Watch what happens—a warm greeting, expressions of kindly concern and good wishes, perhaps. But no action to relieve the obvious physical need. 'What good is that?' asks James (Jas 2:16). 'I will show you my faith by what I do' (Jas 2:18).

How will you find the resources to love the man (or woman) in this situation? How will you afford the meal you might provide, the warm clothes you might give? Here is an opportunity for faith to prove the adequacy of God in the situation. Contact with people with mental handicaps may provide similar opportunities. It is commonly assumed that you need to be some sort of a specialist before you can do anything to help them. Far from it—indeed most people with mental handicaps have parents who were complete novices in the field of specialised care! At the same time it may be that more sensitivity and flexibility, more care as a listener, are essential qualities in those who would be effective in helping them. If such resources are evident in God—as they undoubtedly are—they are also accessible to faith. To respond to a person with a mental handicap I may need wisdom beyond what I now have, and God is delighted to share his with me. Caring for an elderly relative may exhaust my patience, so I need to draw on the infinite patience God shows towards me. Good works express my faith, and expand it as well.

Purpose for living, a duty to love and the nature of faith are but three of many arguments which could be used to show that it is our Christian duty to be socially concerned and active in responding to real need. The case could be argued in terms of the effect it has on other people, giving hope to those who see little to hope for, and bringing comfort into desolation. We could discuss the way it glorifies God. We could use some of the pictures Jesus employed in the Sermon on the Mount to show that we should be like salt and light, like a city on a hill. You probably already feel that what you have read is obvious. Of course it is! Why, then, does it seem so neglected?

Isaiah, the prophet, was given a tough job to do by God. On one occasion he was told to make a public pronouncement about the sins of the people of Israel. They had seriously rebelled against God! (You can read what he wrote in Isaiah 58.) From this you might assume that once again they had abandoned the worship of God in favour of the paganism with which they were surrounded. Not so. They are said to worship God daily; were keen to know God's word; and longed for God to be near them. The average pastor would be delighted to find such enthusiasm in his congregation. What was the problem? Their religion was isolated from their daily lives. They were guilty of injustice and oppression. They neglected to care for the poor or to provide for the hungry.

The problem is still with us. There is still a natural tendency to keep our religion apart from the rest of life. The spiritual and the secular are segregated. One is for Sunday, for quiet times, for meetings. The other is the real and often rather sordid business of living. Which is just what society expects of us. Religion is a private affair—or else it is uncomfortable. God does not share this point of view. It is new life he gives to Christians. He expects it to affect every aspect of our living—family, church, prayer, work, leisure; appreciation of the world about us, the arts, and so on. Jesus came that we might 'have life, and have it to the full' (Jn 10:10), not to impose impoverishing boundaries. He expects our response to human need to be one of the innumerable ways in which our lives will be enriched!

What comes first?

Mention of the relationship between the spiritual and the secular forms a useful bridge to another theme we must explore a little—the upside-down-ness of biblical priorities. The Christian is expected to have a different outlook from that of the non-Christian. Paul told the Christians in Ephesus to 'be made new in the attitude of [their] minds' (Eph 4:23). God's way of thinking seems to reflect different priorities, and ours must come into line with his.

By upside-down-ness I really mean right-side-up-ness! It is we human beings who have got it wrong, having upturned God's standards and priorities. This is hidden from us by virtue of the fact that our natural perspective is normal in the society and culture in which we live.

God is not impressed by bigness, grandness, status or appearance. He is not moved or persuaded on the basis of a person's wealth, a government's political power or a nation's military might. God has a different view of such things, a different range of priorities. Take, for instance, the sort of people he chooses to draw into the life of the church. Writing to the church at Corinth, Paul asked his readers to reflect on this:

> Brothers, think of what you were when you were called. Not many of you were wise by human standards; not many were influential; not many were of noble birth. But God chose the foolish things of the world to shame the wise; God chose the weak things of the world to shame the strong. He chose the lowly things of this world and the despised things—and the things that are not—to nullify the things that are, so that no-one may boast before him (1 Cor 1:26–29).

When you realise that in the Gentile world of his day wisdom was the most highly regarded quality a person could have, then you see how radical Paul was. Certainly the gospel did not fit their accepted norms for wisdom since its 'hero' was killed as a failed rebel leader and his message required humility rather than elevation!

The roots for this sort of thinking lie way back in the Old Testament. It shows that God seems preoccupied with the wrong group of people! He had little time for the impressive civilisations of Babylon and Egypt. Through Moses he told the Israelites that the reason he chose them was not because their nation was significant but because he loved them.

The book of Leviticus was Israel's code of conduct, its legislation from God. The book of Deuteronomy was, in some respects, a commentary on it. Both show a marked preoccupation with four groups of people. The poetic books of Psalms and Proverbs pick up and amplify the theme. Then come the prophets who repeatedly express God's anger that his concern for these groups has not been expressed in the nation's life.

The four groups were the poor, the fatherless, the widow and 'the stranger in the land'.

Why was special consideration needed for these four groups of people? As the nation stood on the threshold of what was to be their new land, Moses reminded them that once there they would have a new basis for social economics. Land would provide security for each family and would be held by them in perpetuity. If it was sold it would revert to the family in the Year of Jubilee. These four groups could find themselves outside that economic system, or at least inadequately protected by it. A family might sell their land to pay debts; an orphan might be excluded from a right to the title of the property until coming of age; a widow might lose her husband's land to another relative; and the 'stranger' was a foreigner having no natural right to land in Israel. As the economy was based on agriculture, these four groups had no means of providing for themselves, no land on which to grow their food, no security. They were thus vulnerable to exploitation and injustice as well as to poverty and starvation.

God took it upon himself to protect their rights. Legislation was embedded in the nation's life to safeguard their interests (Deut 24:12–18). At harvest time they were to be given freedom to glean fields and vines, and the harvesters were to leave them sufficient to make their gleaning worthwhile (Lev 19:9–10; Deut 24:19–22)! Every third year the tithes of the crops were to be given to these groups, providing them with longer term help and the prospect of climbing out of depressing poverty (Deut 14:28–29). Specific rules were also given to ensure that their spiritual welfare was safeguarded too (Ex 12:48; Deut 16:11,14).

Not only were these controls put on social life; positive encouragement was given, to those with the means to do so, to share with the disadvantaged.

> Blessed is he who has regard for the weak; the Lord delivers him in times of trouble. The Lord will protect him and preserve his life; he will bless him in the land (Ps 41:1–2).

> He who is kind to the poor lends to the Lord, and he will reward him for what he has done (Prov 19:17).

God undertook to defend their cause:

> He stands at the right hand of the needy one, to save his life from those who condemn him (Ps 109:31).

> I know the Lord secures justice for the poor and upholds the cause of the needy (Ps 140:12).

> Do not exploit the poor because they are poor and do not crush the needy in court, for the Lord will take up their case and will plunder those who plunder them (Prov 22:22–23).

The prophets were God's spokesmen when, instead of receiving protection, the poor were exploited by the rich. The divine priorities are quite clear, as is the fact that they are different from our own!

Nowhere is upside-down-ness more obvious than in the

life and ministry of Jesus. You see it in the fact that God the Son became a human being. Coming as a baby was itself an identification with insignificance. This was demonstrated the more so in the choice of his parents, the place of his birth and those who were first to welcome his arrival—the shepherds. The herald of his public ministry was a hermit, and his companions during the three years he travelled from obscurity to notoriety were ordinary working men and women. The emphasis of his ministry was:

> to proclaim freedom for the prisoners and recovery of sight for the blind, to release the oppressed, to proclaim the year of the Lord's favour (Lk 4:18–19).

So much for the evidence. It is overwhelming—and there is a good deal more which could be added. If we were less familiar with it we would be staggered at this consistent underplay of human greatness and the elevation of the marginalised. The challenge to us in our time is to adopt the same outlook and attitude. It flies in the face of our culture and our inclinations, and it is these influences which have shaped much of our church life and affected our Christian priorities.

> The fact is that our whole civilisation suggests to us a false scale of values. It accords positive value to all that is strong, and negative value to all that is weak. It is shameful to be weak, sensitive, pitiable, or affectionate.[8]

But, equally, our culture is out of step with God.

Now let us bring this to bear on our central theme. We are considering people who are unlikely to make a major contribution to learning or science. They will not be in the lead for beauty, agility, artistic skill or physical prowess. They will not be actors of note, politicians of significance, television presenters, or wealthy entrepreneurs. All of the categories which our society esteems are likely to exclude them. The question this provokes is: 'What matters?' In the larger context of time and eternity who will remember Joan Collins or Richard Burton, Terry Wogan or Ruby Wax, Lord Hansford or Laura Ashley, Margaret Thatcher or Mikael Gorbachev? God will certainly be applying different criteria from those which elevate people like these. And those criteria make it possible that heaven's list of 'the greats' will include people who have been disregarded by their contemporaries. Some of them, I am absolutely sure, will be people with mental handicaps. I have met some of them!

In seeking to bring our attitudes into line with God's we will have to adjust our outlook in respect of people with mental handicaps. If we reject the idea that to be weak is shameful then there is no reason to look down on those who, by virtue of their intellectual limitations, are weak—socially, politically, economically. In fact, if we are also to reverse the disregard they currently suffer we will have to exercise positive discrimination in their favour. We will not only have to stop thinking in the old way, we will have to do something to counteract the negative effects of our previous attitudes. Challenging stuff, this! Later chapters will suggest some ways in which we can put this into effect.

It is high time this chapter came to an end, but we have not quite reached our destination. The impression may have been given that we must see good where there is none, that we must pretend that there is actually some value in people when such value is so slight as to be not worth considering— whether they be poor, widowed or have a mental handicap. In particular some attempt must be made to show the worth of people with mental handicaps in response to the arguments put forward here. If they are to be more present in our communities, if God doesn't seem enthusiastic to heal them, we must conclude that there is some reason for people with mental handicaps to be here among us. The search for some meaning and purpose is understandable.

But it is also elusive. What may be true of one person may not be true of another. An explanation which fits in one setting may be out of place in another. We may be able to offer a way of viewing mental handicap which will help us to value people with mental handicaps in a variety of settings. This, in turn, will help us to cope with their inevitable presence in the future.

> Unlike some disorders, it is virtually certain that there will always be [people with mental handicaps] unless all fetuses at risk were aborted, and all infants and children who appear to have retarded mental development were put to death. ...their timeless presence, I believe, is by divine design. . . . I believe the design is more likely intended to confront human beings endlessly with themselves and their own nature and essence.[9]

One word which sums up that confrontation is simplicity. It is the result of impaired intellectual function. Everything is pared down to the point that each can cope with what is happening in his environment.

Simplicity is a virtue, not a failing. And it is a rare virtue in our world, where technology has invaded every aspect of our existence so that consumerism is preoccupied with gadgets. As we speed along the road from our electronically protected house, in our computer controlled car, to our centrally heated office to sign word-processed letters, we pass a man on the pavement waiting to cross over to the other side. Patiently he waits for us, and others, to hurry on our way. But he stands there as a living reminder of the essentials of our existence. His home is simply furnished. His days are almost filled by the tasks of caring for himself. He cannot drive, nor is he employed. He is despised by many for his mental handicap. But he is, and what he is reminds us of what we are too. We need that reminder. We need to see beyond the full and flashy lives we lead to recognise what is our real self.

> In the handicapped we can discern the human condition. We are none of us 'perfect'. We share the same basic needs—food, drink, sleep, love. . . . We have the same instinctive desire for life, the

same ultimate end in death, the same frailty, the same vulnerability. We need to sense this identification with those who reveal, sometimes very poignantly, what the human condition really is. We are all in need of grace.[10]

That simplicity has a 'gentling' effect on others. For people with mental handicaps, friendships are relatively unsophisticated. Most will accept a person simply for being himself. Time and again I have seen this have a life-changing effect in people who have themselves suffered rejection.

There are strong links between two Christian residential homes in the Reading area. Helena House is a home for people with mental handicaps. Yeldall Manor is a rehabilitation centre for men who have been addicted to drugs for many years. In the course of the rehabilitation programme the men have the opportunity to do voluntary work as part of the process of returning to normal living. Some have been sent to Helena House for this purpose. Often it has brought dramatic change in the former addict's life. They are accepted as friends, no questions asked. No pretence; no threat. Tough men, some with a record of violent crime and imprisonment, are made gentler, kinder by their contact with uncomplicated people.

Many a church or housegroup is grateful for the simplicity with which problems are turned to prayer by Christians with a mental handicap. Peter is one such.

He is now a member of a home group and has made significant contributions to the development of the group's prayer life, first by always having somebody to ask prayer for, and often bringing Bible study to an end by telling the group to pray. . . . His first response to trouble and illness that he sees is to pray for people, often with them directly, and at various times in the last few years he seems to have had a particular ministry to people in the fellowship who are dying.[11]

If only we could regain something of that simplicity in all of us! Some writers have referred to this as the prophetic role of people with mental handicaps. A prophet is one who speaks to men for God. Perhaps it is a fair description. Maybe the thing we most need to hear from God in our bustling, sound-filled world is simply that we are, and what we are is more important than what we have and the things with which we are so often preoccupied.

> What mankind needs in our day, if it is to escape the catastrophe towards which it is being led by our rationalist and technical civilisation, is just these qualities of kindness, conscience, emotion, sensitiveness, beauty and intuition which lie repressed and asleep deep in the hearts of those whom that civilisation despises.[12]

> They can effect in us a change of heart, a new set of values, a new perspective. They can show us what true humanity is. There is a sense in which we are all handicapped, we are all vulnerable, and far from perfect. We need to let the reality of handicap be a critique of our illusions, our ambitions, our much-vaunted achievements.[13]

Why should I care? The question must seem irrelevant to us now. Indeed you may be left with a more disturbing question: Why has it taken me so long to care? Why have I been so slow to share God's commitment to people who are disadvantaged? How much have I missed? How far is my part of the Christian community impoverished by its disregard of dependent people?

But there is need for realism. To rush in on a wave of emotion will bring us crashing into issues which will smash our fragile, new-found zeal into a thousand pieces. The enrichment available is at the price of grappling with some big questions.

Notes

[1] C.S. Lewis, *The Problem of Pain* (Fontana: London, 1965), p 28.

[2] *Ibid*, pp 34–35.

[3] J.W. Wenham, *The Goodness of God* (Inter-Varsity Press: Leicester, 1974), p 46.

[4] *Ibid*, p 83.

[5] J. Stott, *Issues Facing Christians Today* (Marshalls: Basingstoke, 1984), p 2.

[6] R. Pierce Beaver, quoted *ibid*, pp 5–6.

[7] Stott, *ibid*, pp 14–15.

[8] P. Tournier, *The Strong and the Weak* (Highland Books: UK, 1984), p 163.

[9] W. Wolfensberger, *The Prophetic Voice and Presence of Mentally Retarded People in the World Today* (Unpublished paper, 1976), pp 8–9.

[10] F. Young, *Face to Face* (T & T Clark: Edinburgh, 1990), p 106.

[11] N. Smith, 'A Special Ministry', *Christian Arena*, vol 42 (June 1989): pp 8–9.

[12] Tournier, *op cit*, p 165.

[13] Young, *op cit*, p 182.

8
What's the Answer?

It depends what the question is?

There's more than one!

Ask them. Let's see if there are answers.

Well, 'Should they be allowed?', for example.

What do you mean, 'Should they be allowed?'

Should mentally handicapped people be allowed to live? After all, they cause a lot of suffering, and they suffer themselves. Isn't it better that they aren't born?

That's some question! Any more?

Yes, wouldn't they be better off dead? I mean, when their parents can't care for them any more and they have to leave their home to live elsewhere, perhaps in an institution. It's such a terrible shock for them. Wouldn't it be better for them to die in the security of their own home?

Some security!

Mental handicap raises some profound and searching moral questions. The answers affect the way people live and die. We must look at some of these practical issues and face the difficult questions. And in respect of people with mental handicaps few questions are more difficult than those relating to sex!

Issues of life and love

Ought we to recognise the sexuality of people with mental handicap, because it might lead to their having children?

Which puts the issue rather bluntly but effectively sums up the concerns which many have. In recent years the courts have been asked to decide whether or not a woman with a mental handicap should be sterilised. It is a moral dilemma we must think about. But there are wider issues before we come to that particular difficulty.

Reactions to sex and people with mental handicaps are likely to fall into three broad categories:
1 Those who argue that people with mental handicaps have the right to the same sexual experiences as other people. They must receive help to enjoy these rights.
2 Those who regard people with mental handicaps as asexual—as having no sexual urge and therefore not requiring sexual fulfilment.
3 Those who regard people with mental handicaps as oversexed and liable to interfere with children, rape women or engage in homosexual acts.

Not surprisingly, therefore, the issue is fraught with prejudice, fear and misunderstanding. When one takes account of the abuse to which many people with mental handicaps have been subjected, both in institutions and outside, and the neglect of their deeply felt needs, it is no wonder that this is a difficult matter for them as well as for us. From a Christian perspective none of the three categories mentioned above is acceptable, but developing one which is in harmony with the Bible is quite a challenge.

We have already laid some foundations on which to build. Sexuality is part of being made in God's likeness. Do you recall what we quoted from Genesis?

So God created man in his own image, in the image of God he created him; male and female he created them (Gen 1:27).

It is fascinating to realise that maleness and femaleness are both expressions of the divine nature. It is when they take human form they are different. Men and women are both like God but they are dissimilar from one another. Once again we are looking at differentness—and as someone has said, 'Vive la différence!'

Masculinity and femininity are expressions of difference between men and women. They show themselves in physical and emotional characteristics. They have little to do with who keeps house or who drives the tractor, but everything to do with how we relate to each other. All the issues which affect your sexuality affect also a person with a mental handicap of the same sex as you. They may be more or less sensitive to them than you are, but so may I be. They are as varied in their sexuality as people in society at large. How it is expressed will vary from one to another and be as much influenced by their moral awareness, their upbringing, their self-conciousness as would any one else. Fulfilment is as much a need for them as for the rest of us.

Relationships are a key aspect of sexuality. We relate to others man to man, woman to woman, man to woman, woman to man. Those relationships range from casual contact between customer and check-out operator, to the intimate bond between husband and wife. Coping with this wide range of personal interaction is part of the sophisticated expression of our male or female personalities. How well we cope will be helped by our positive experiences and hindered by our negative experiences. The more we practise relationships, the more we will be able to cope with such diversity. The more successful we are, the more we gain respect from others and develop confidence in ourselves.

It is easy to imagine that a person with a mental handicap may well find himself in difficulties with such a complex range of relationships. Suppose that from an early age his parents have felt disappointment at his handicap; that will have undermined his sense of self-worth. He will have suffered discrimination at school, been jeered at by other children, avoided, excluded or ignored. Small wonder if such a person has problems in relating to other people, either by avoidance or by overstepping the boundaries of propriety. It would be hard enough for a person who has learned the necessary social graces. How much harder for one whose learning ability is impaired. We must help such a person rediscover his value by warm and supportive friendship. This is one way in which to express the 'love your neighbour' ethic of the New Testament, and is the first stage in helping individuals to come to terms with their sexual needs. They do not exist in a vacuum.

No problem so far, but what about sex and people with mental handicap? Young men with mental handicaps struggle with feelings and fantasies, and young women with infatuations. Both may make slower progress to maturity, but we would be unwise to assume that sexual development does not take place.

The expression of sexual desires and their fulfilment are good and acceptable within the clear framework provided by the Bible. It does not make any distinctions on the grounds of intellectual ability or inability. The enrichment which is possible and the constraints which it lays down are relevant to people of all sorts. It is not surprising that people with mental handicaps fall in love—indeed they are often required to live in such close proximity with each other that this is quite likely to happen. Nor should this be regarded as strange or in some way undesirable. There is also the possibility that a non-handicapped person might marry a person with a mental handicap. It has happened and proved successful. It is a beautiful thing when two human beings find themselves in a new way through the love of another person.

The body of man is made to be united with the body of woman. The psychology of one is complementary to the psychology of the other. They are created to be companions and friends; they are made to have children and to educate them together. The gifts of one harmonise with the gifts of the other; their differences are enriching.[1]

Can this really apply to people regardless of ability? It is difficult to say that it does not.

Between two people with mental handicaps a romance may be a more or less platonic friendship. Holding hands while watching television may be the nearest it comes to intimacy. But if they are capable of a deeper relationship they may wish it to have a sexual expression and for that to happen the Bible provides the context of marriage.

Marriage! For people with mental handicaps? Surely that can't be right! They couldn't cope. What if there are children? It's not natural. These are typical reactions, but are they right?

Let's try to look at the matter unemotionally. John and Mary have fallen in love. John attended his brother's wedding last year. Mary has twice been bridesmaid to her sisters. Both John and Mary have seen what a difference marriage has made to their siblings. It is not surprising that they should regard it as the usual thing for two people who are in love to want to get married. And they are in love themselves. They are committed to each other. But they also have mental handicaps. Why should not those who support them enable them to enjoy the enrichment most of us take for granted? Would their relationship fulfil the purpose for which marriage is given?

The purpose of marriage is a primary question in this discussion. If marriage is primarily for procreation—having children—then there are several issues to be considered. But is child-bearing essential to marriage? It is worth looking back at Genesis—after all, marriage was God's idea in the first place!

God created Eve to be a companion for Adam: 'It is not good for the man to be alone' (Gen 2:18). There was no other creature who could meet Adam's need for friendship. Eve was made to be perfectly complementary to Adam, to be his equal without whom he was somehow incomplete and unfulfilled.

Married couples usually find that their companionship is the greatest benefit of their relationship, and the aspect most missed if the marriage breaks down. It is possible within marriage to discover a level of security and acceptance that is not possible in any other form of relationship.

Closeness, acceptance and security are especially desirable for people who have suffered alienation and rejection to an extent most of us would find intolerable. To deny them such a possibility by refusing in principle marriage between people with mental handicaps is biblically questionable and exceedingly harsh.

What if they were to have children? The first couple were told to 'Be fruitful and increase' (Gen 1:28). A similar command was given to Noah and his wife after the devastation of the Flood. God had made the world to be a home for people with whom he wanted a relationship. So it is no surprise that this required that there should be people. And people make people, if you follow my meaning!

Is there a limit to the 'creation mandate'? Statistics suggest that the world is now more than 'filled' and might even be close to its maximum population level. The challenge we are considering is whether a couple entering marriage must intend to have children. Are measures to prevent conception sometimes (in the way many Western couples use contraception) more acceptable than preventing conception always? These are surely matters on which most of us would hesitate to lay down rules for other couples.

Yet such rules are often laid down for people with mental handicaps. Those who believe that procreation is an essential expression of the marriage relationship would forbid marriage to a couple who, because of their mental handicap, do not intend to have children. Which is a hard judgement on them when made by those who are enjoying the privilege of family life.

How should we face the possibility that people with mental handicaps might have children if they married? Preparation for marriage would have to involve the couple in clear and explicit instruction about sex. And they would have to discuss and consider contraception. They would also have to be helped to understand that babies are different from dollies.

They must be shown how significant, and at times onerous(!), are the responsibilities of parenthood. At the end of the day the couple may decide that both marriage and parenthood are what they want. It is possible that they may bear a child which also has a handicap, but not necessarily so. Those involved in the care and support of the couple will have to decide whether they can sustain that support, and discuss that decision and its implications with the couple.

The point of raising the matter here is to encourage discussion. Answers will vary from one situation to another. The answer may lie in the direction of sterilisation for the man or the woman. That is certainly an option, and if it were the wish of the couple then it is an acceptable option. If it is not their wish, should sterilisation be imposed? Which brings us to another contemporary debate.

The issue of sterilisation came forcefully into public view in 1987. Sunderland Borough Council made a teenage girl a ward of court in order to arrange for her to be sterilised. There were two reasons for this: first, Jeanette (as she was known to the court) had a moderate degree of mental handicap; second, she was shortly to become eighteen years of age. The young woman was considered incapable of giving consent to such an operation, as would be required once she passed her eighteenth birthday. The three Appeal Court judges agreed to the operation while she was still a minor 'for her own good'.

The Times ponderously affirmed 'their decision was correct'. Not everyone agreed. Numerous voices spoke out against it, including a spokesman for the Mental Health Foundation and the National Council for Civil Liberties. Professor Michael Freeman said that the decision was 'Nazi, almost'. Sir Brian Rix of MENCAP expressed strong opposition to the decision. The British Association of Social Workers joined the chorus of opposition by saying, 'We have difficulty in understanding how such extreme measures might be justified.' *Community Care*, a magazine serving the social work profession, reported 'widespread alarm' at the decision.

And in the swirl of publicity surrounding the case it became clear that imposed sterilisations had taken place without the consent of the courts on girls with mental handicaps. However, when the case went to the House of Lords on appeal, five Law Lords gave their unanimous approval for the operation to proceed.

The question left hanging in the air was what would have happened if Jeanette was over eighteen years of age. By the end of 1988 this question also was before the courts. This time it concerned a lady of thirty-five years of age living in a mental handicap hospital near Reading. She became known to the court as 'F'.

It may be inevitable in cases like this that the level of the person's disability is unclear. Those requesting the action wish to show that the person is so limited in understanding that she is incapable of decision in the matter. The courts have little contact with people with mental handicaps and are therefore likely to assume low expectations of any person described as having a mental handicap! F was rated as having 'a general mental capacity of a four or five year old'.

This case was brought by the mother of F and opposed by the health authority. It appears that F was having a sexual relationship with another resident in the hospital. No one was sure whether it involved sexual intercourse but this was thought possible, even probable. Contraception was believed to pose a health risk. Pregnancy would be 'an unmitigated disaster' according to the judge in the High Court. The issue went to appeal and the House of Lords upheld the decision of the lower court—an operation could proceed to sterilise F without the necessity of her giving consent. It was 'in her best interests' to do so.

About the earlier case a *Guardian* editorial had said:

> The decision to sterilise is bad for several reasons. It is bad because it asserts that the courts really can divide the population into those who are fit to reproduce and those who are not. . . . It is bad because its finality denies the possibility of change or

improvement in the person to be sterilised. . . . It is bad because it is a judgment with more than a hint of expediency about it, the expediency which says there aren't enough social workers around to care for such people any more. . . . It is bad also because the finality of sterilisation is not the only available solution. . . . They have established a precedent which inevitably means that more sterilisations will be considered.[2]

And so they were!

The discussion on sterilisation will become obscure unless we keep in mind that it is not about whether or not a person with a mental handicap may or may not be sterilised. It is about whether such an intrusive operation should be allowed without the individual's consent for a condition which is not life threatening in circumstances which are not an emergency.

What made [the sterilisation of F] a legal case, rather than merely medical or social, was that under common law no one can interfere with the body of another adult without their consent, except in an emergency.[3]

The key issue is this: given that the relationship was taking place and would continue to do so; given that it would be undesirable for F to become pregnant; was the best course open to her carers to arrange serious surgery without her approval so as to make any incidence of intercourse 'safe'? (Which itself begs any number of questions!) In answering this question we need to ask other questions.

First, why should F be the person to be sterilised? A vasectomy is a simpler operation. Her partner, it seemed, was more able and might have been asked to consent to minor surgery.

Second, was it really impossible to gain F's consent? In the courts she was described as both severely mentally handicapped and able to consent to and enjoy a sexual relationship. Psychologists in mental handicap have expressed the view that, given time and skill, it is possible to enable people with profound mental handicaps to share in choices about their lives. An officer of the health authority told me that they believed this was the case with F, but her mother disagreed with them.

Third, are Jeanette and F any better off? The answer must be 'No!' Admittedly they cannot now get pregnant, but that advantage was at an enormous cost to them. They are now more than ever vulnerable to sexual exploitation and abuse, with its added possibility of contracting Aids.

Our society does not sufficiently appreciate how much its life has been made complex by abandoning our Christian heritage. If this heritage had been upheld the problems would not walk off stage, but it would be possible to view them within a moral framework which is meaningful and enriching for society. Seeing people as made in God's image would challenge our inclination to exploit those who are weaker. Seeing sex as part of a relationship rather than its prime purpose would urge us to find ways to enable dependent people to enjoy the companionship and love for which sexuality is an ideal expression.

The secular process of the courts has, in fact, created even greater dilemmas for us. They touch the lives of people who consider themselves to be 'normal' but result in horrendous measures against people they consider to be 'non-normal' in ways that make enforced sterilisation seem almost acceptable in contrast.

Issues of life and death

Every scientific advance brings with it more difficult decisions for those on the front line of treating illness and disease. Often the questions are resolved not by medical possibilities but financial considerations. Does the doctor use the only life-support machine available for the elderly man suffering a stroke or the youngster brought in from a motor cycle accident? How many hip replacements can be done for the price of a heart and lung transplant? It is not surprising that such 'acute' services are often seen as more important than responding to the needs of people with mental handicaps.

If you want to raise the emotional temperature of a discussion just bring up subjects like abortion, infanticide and euthanasia. Numerous books have been written on each of these topics, setting out opposing views with passion and conviction. We too have to address them, but you will have to look elsewhere for a thorough-going debate. Our concern here will be to consider the implications of these vital questions only as they affect people with mental handicaps.

Should they be allowed to be born?

In 1967 abortion was legalised in Britain. At the outset the categories were carefully defined. With the passage of time they were interpreted increasingly freely and by the late 1980s several attempts were being made to restrict the categories and time limits for abortion.

David Steel introduced his Private Members Bill in 1967 with the help of the Abortion Law Reform Association which, at the time, had only 1,000 members. The general climate of opinion among the public and the medical profession was one of opposition. The Act was intended to allow abortions for serious medical and social reasons and to restrict illegal abortions, which were said to be the cause of death for numbers of women. The time limit for an abortion was set at twenty-eight weeks from conception. The Act also permitted abortion if there was 'substantial risk that if the child were born it would suffer from such physical or mental abnormalities as to be seriously handicapped'.

There has been a strong undercurrent of opposition to the repeal or amendment of the Act. In 1988 David Alton's Bill came within a whisker of becoming law, only to be defeated by a procedural device exploited by a minority. Amendment was finally achieved in April 1990 during the passage of the Human Fertilisation and Embryo Bill. This Bill superseded that of 1967 and introduced serious freedoms in the realm of research on human embryos. It also made it impossible in future for doctors to face criminal charges for killing a baby in the womb that could be born alive. And it reduced the time limit for abortion to twenty-four weeks. Its most alarming clause allows abortion if there is substantial risk that the child will be seriously disabled, and such abortion may take place at any time up to the moment of birth.

What difference does it make if the unborn baby has a handicap? Clearly some see this as an important issue. It swayed many of the Members of Parliament who had voted against more liberal measures on other clauses of the Bill. It also sways many others, Christian and non-Christian, who are otherwise unhappy about abortion.

At one time, of course, it could not have been an issue because there was no means of knowing whether the unborn baby had any conditions that would handicap its life. Nowadays there is a veritable battery of tests and methods whereby defects in the baby can be known at various stages in its development. Some disabilities show up in ultrasound scanning of the baby in the womb. Foetoscopy, involving the insertion into the womb of a probe with a light, enables the doctor to see deformities as small as a cleft palate. Some disabilities are shown up by tests on fluid taken from the amniotic sac surrounding the baby, or by removing small pieces of tissue from the sac. Some can show up in a simple blood test on the mother, or at least alert doctors to the need for more thorough tests.

There are limitations to these amazing pre-birth tests. For example, they can show that a child has Down's syndrome, but they cannot predict to what degree intelligence will be affected. There are some dangers to the baby and the mother from the tests. Infection may be introduced into the womb. Miscarriage may even be induced.

Once armed with the knowledge that the baby is handicapped the medical practitioner is then in a position to advise—and, often, to pressurise—the mother to have an abortion. And, if she has consented to the test, it seems logical to expect her to agree. After all, every parent wants a perfect baby—and who will blame them for that!

An increasingly significant argument in favour of the abortion of babies with disabilities is the subsequent cost of care and treatment. In 1989 Professor Bob Williamson, leader of the cystic fibrosis research unit at St Mary's Hospital Medical School, spoke on behalf of the Royal College of Physicians at the launch of a report on pre-natal screening and diagnosis. He argued that the screening would cost less than £1 whereas a cystic fibrosis child costs £10,000 a year to treat. Similar advances in tests for Down's syndrome are advocated on the same basis. We shall hear this argument more often as our society listens to daily reports on national economic indicators and is concerned at the effects of cuts in services for health and education.

Should they be allowed to live?

Once the baby is born one expects that the risk to its life is over. In the main that is the case, but it would be unwise to assume that the baby is safe and secure. (After all, one could hardly find a more secure place than the womb!) Speaking in the House of Lords debate on the Human Fertilisation and Embryo Bill the Duke of Norfolk quoted Professor Glanville Williams on this matter:

> When a live fetus is removed in the course of an abortion, the fetus upon being removed becomes a legal person and is fully protected by law . . . because it is live extraction from the woman that endows the fetus with legal personality.[4]

If that is the case it not only speaks to the issue of abortion but also to infanticide. Infanticide is the killing of a baby, and there is abundant evidence that this is happening more and more widely in respect of babies found to have handicaps at birth. Not that it is a particularly new practice.

In 1981 the issue came to the fore in the trial of Dr Leonard Arthur. He was accused of the attempted murder of John

Pearson, a baby with Down's syndrome. In spite of his handicap, and some slight heart and lung defects, the Home Office pathologist was convinced that the child had an 80 per cent chance of survival. That he did not survive was due to the 'treatment' prescribed by the pediatrician, Dr Arthur.

> The case for the prosecution was that the doctor prescribed a course of non-treatment by the administration of the drug DF118 which suppresses appetite and impairs breathing. There was no apparent reason to administer the drug.[5]

The baby's notes were marked, 'Parents do not wish the baby to survive. Nursing care only.' After three and a half days, during which he showed increasing distress, John Pearson died.

> The case [for the prosecution] was a strong one, not least because Leonard Arthur had admitted that if parents rejected a mentally handicapped child—which they had—it was honest and ethical from his standpoint that the child was better off dead.[6]

During the course of the trial Dr Arthur's position was supported by a strong lobby of high ranking pediatricians who stated that it was acceptable 'to invoke a regime of starvation and sedation to quickly speed the demise of the handicapped child'. Furthermore, critics of the practice were accused of 'ignorance and misunderstanding of how the science and art of pediatrics is practised'![7]

At about the same time there was a further case which received widespread publicity in respect of another baby with Down's syndrome, a little girl known as Alexandra. She suffered from a duodenal obstruction which required immediate surgery, but for which her parents refused to give consent. The doctor called in the hospital social workers and the child was made a ward of court. Consent was given for the operation to proceed. Doctors at Great Ormond Street refused to operate. The operation was successfully conducted at Hammersmith Hospital.

Since that time there have been several other cases before the courts to decide whether or not a handicapped child should live. The balance of judgement has not always been in their favour, though there has been a distinct shift away from encouraging the 'starvation/sedation' regime used by Dr Arthur.

It is, however, disconcerting to find that for a considerable time the medical profession has favoured non-treatment for handicapped babies. In 1975 at a conference on Ethical Issues in Neonatal Intensive Care held in California, out of a panel of twenty, seventeen members agreed that it would be right to kill a 'self-sustaining infant.'[8] In a 1982 survey by *Hospital Doctor* (a British magazine), 200 doctors, 77 per cent of consultants asked, and 71 per cent of junior doctors supported a doctor's right to determine the survival of severely handicapped babies.

Severe disability or mental handicap evident at birth may result in parents having to share in deciding whether or not the baby should live. Where the decision is for non-treatment the method used is usually starvation. Dr Lorber, a specialist in spina bifida, suggests the following approach:

> It is essential that those who are not treated should not live long. It is imperative, therefore, that non-treatment should really be non-treatment, not just no operation. Nothing should be done to prolong life.[9]

Baby Doe, an American boy with Down's syndrome, lived for six days. Lawyers argued about his future while doctors withheld treatment—no food other than injections of barbiturates and morphine. The incident caused a national outrage and led to changes in legislation. The Dr Arthur case received a similar degree of publicity in Britain but had a different outcome. Doctors are now less inhibited in following his example.

It is not surprising, therefore, that the message is getting through to parents that they don't need to cope with a handicapped child.

In interview, Dr Gordon Stirrat, clinical Reader in Nuffield Department of Obstetrics and Gynaecology at the University of Oxford, remarked that, 'In today's abortion mentality we are beginning to see amongst women a consumer attitude towards their pregnancies—the line is when you order a baby you order a good one and if it's no good, you send it back.'[10]

Should we help them die?

So far our focus has been on the unborn or the newborn. Similar arguments are used in respect of adults with mental handicaps. The solution for their long-term care has been found—in euthanasia. So far as we are aware this has only been canvassed as distinct from being practised. However, it is being suggested with increasing seriousness.

I first bumped into the issue almost by accident. A 'medical' friend asked me to speak on the subject of euthanasia at a meeting she was organising. I was surprised at the request because I knew nothing much about the subject. She was surprised at my ignorance since she knew it to be a discussion topic as a possible solution to the long-term care of people with mental handicaps. So I began to look at the issue more closely. (I then wrote a book entitled *Too Soon to Die*.)

In 1978 an article appeared in a social work journal, written by a prominent social work figure, Dame Eileen Younghusband. It was entitled 'The Right to Die'. Along the way the author posed the problem like this:

> The severely handicapped person is as vulnerable as a child. Even if he is secure and well-cared for in his family setting, there is often the gnawing question 'What will happen to him when we die?' Is the answer years maybe in the backwards of a subnormality hospital or, if there is no better alternative, to be permitted to die peacefully at his parents' wish with his security still around him?[11]

Nowadays, with the large-scale closure of mental handicap hospitals, there may not even be hope of the 'backwards' to which Dame Eileen referred. With drastically reduced funding by local and national government, the parents of a mentally handicapped person have more reason than ever to be concerned about the long-term care of their son or daughter. That person is more likely to outlive parents than was the case, say, thirty years ago. Some adults with mental handicaps have picked up their parents' anxiety and are themselves concerned about their future. Where will I live? Will I like it? Will other people live there too? Will I like them? Will they like me? Can I take my cat/armchair/hi-fi/magazines, etc?

Over the years I have heard numerous and tragic stories of people with mental handicaps finding their parent dead. Vigilant neighbours heard a mentally handicapped lady crying next door and found her in bed alongside her dead mother. A man with Down's syndrome found his mother 'asleep' on the kitchen floor. Hunger drove him next door after two days of bewilderment. There is an issue to be faced—and Dame Eileen's proposal offers one solution!

Nor is it only a question as to how to provide the person with a mental handicap with long-term care. Can that person hope for an acceptable quality of life? There may be real obstacles to that inherent in the person's handicap. There may also be difficulties arising from non-acceptance by society. Without question a person with a mental handicap will have a different way of life, being more dependent, less likely to own property, limited in income, perhaps unable to read, drive or even walk. Whether that individual's life is different in quality will depend on a number of factors which must vary from person to person. If it does fall below a certain standard should he or she be spared old age? Many are now saying 'Yes' to that question.

> Traditional ethics based on the sanctity of life—which was the classical doctrine of medical idealism in its prescientific phases—must give way to a code of ethics of the quality of life.[12]

The likely cost of providing for dependent people is an increasingly live issue with the cutbacks seen in public services in recent years. Combined with the fact that people with mental handicaps are unlikely to have made any 'economic' contribution to their society, this makes them more vulnerable than those who retire after years as tax-payers. Obnoxious as the idea seems at first, the burden of care is very costly. A severely handicapped person in a residential setting may require a level of support which costs £30,000 a year. Assume that begins at twenty years of age and continues until his death at sixty. Increase the figure annually for inflation and before long tens of thousands of pounds become hundreds of thousands, and eventually the million mark is left behind. Just for one person—and there are tens of thousands like this. If you add on the cost of buying or building property for this purpose, again one must think in tens of thousands of pounds for each place provided.

Such considerations make even the humane and compassionate person wonder whether there are other solutions.

More than a decade ago, Wolfensberger warned:

> The stage appears set for another assault upon the severely and even moderately afflicted. Euthanasia is being committed in various forms and guises—and not rarely at all.[13]

So what is the answer?

Before launching into specifics, it is important to note a modern trend.

> A new medicine is arising to challenge, and seek to displace, the old, with in the place of healing as its supreme objective a fluid and undefined notion of the relief of suffering—which can encompass even the taking of life.[14]

The prevention and relief of suffering has become the preoccupation on both sides of the doctor's desk, for the professional and the patient. 'Please can you give me something to take away my cough/pain/sickness/tiredness, etc.' The shift from the essentially Christian view of medicine as a healing art has taken place almost unobserved. But it is this newer outlook which now pervades our thinking, and nowhere more so than in respect of abortion, infanticide and euthanasia. How should we respond?

First we need to be clear as to what we are discussing. Many will agree that human life is to be respected, but are we talking about human beings when we speak of people with mental handicaps? The advocates of euthanasia question whether humanness can be attributed to those who have a mental handicap. Following research into the literature on involuntary euthanasia, Evelyn Lusthaus wrote:

> In almost all cases where involuntary euthanasia is proposed, the rationalisations provided are based on the idea that the people who would be killed are not really people. Persons who have mental retardation and other impairments are being defined as subhuman. . . . It is proposed that individuals are not fully human unless they have certain features that are required for humanness. . . . At the top of the list is intelligence.[15]

J. Fletcher wrote:

> Any individual of the species homo sapiens who falls below the IQ-40 mark in a standard Stanford-Binet test . . . is questionably a person; below the 20–mark, not a person. . . .[16]

Peter Singer, an Australian professor of philosophy, went still further when he wrote:

> We will not regard as sacrosanct the life of each and every member of our species, no matter how limited its capacity for intelligent or even conscious life may be. If we compare a severely defective human infant with a non-human animal, a dog or pig, for example, we will often find the non-human to have superior capacities, both actual and potential, for rationality, self-conciousness, communication, and anything else that can plausibly be considered morally significant.[17]

You may now understand why, in an earlier chapter, so much time was spent establishing what makes people people. The arguments do not need repetition here, other than to affirm once again that human beings are what they are because they are made in the image of God.

Now we must face a further question: When does human life begin? If it begins prior to birth then the very vulnerability of the baby renders it the more deserving of our protection and care.

There are four options as to when we recognise the fetus or baby as a human being:

1 it is a human being from the moment of conception;
2 it becomes a human being at some point between conception and birth;
3 it becomes a human being when it is born;
4 it becomes a human being at some point subsequent to birth.

Let's look at them in reverse order. The extreme of this view was expressed by Francis Crick, a Nobel prize-winner in medicine and physiology, who wrote:

> No newborn infant should be declared human until it has passed certain tests regarding its genetic endowment. If it fails these tests, it forfeits the right to live.[18]

If the moment of birth (as option 3 above) is the point at which the baby is acceptable as a human being, one is faced with some awkward questions. What should be its status just before it is born? How should it be regarded if it is delivered by 'unnatural' means, like surgery? If it is unduly late in being born does it still remain non-human and therefore vulnerable to rejection? What happens at birth is very significant, but it is only the realisation of what has been possible for nine months. The location of the baby has changed. So has its relationship to its mother. But it is in most respects what it was immediately before its delivery. Why should it now be thought to be human whereas moments before it was not?

The arguments are similar against trying to fix some point between conception and birth (as option 2 above) as the time when the baby becomes human. The most commonly suggested moment is at around fourteen days, when the embryo is implanted into the wall of the uterus. This, it is said, marks a most significant change in the development of the person. It certainly is significant, but it does not change the embryo into a baby or the baby into a human. It changes the relationship of the baby/embryo to its environment. It is a stage in its development and growth, of which there are many in the course of a pregnancy. To mark out one such stage as a change into humanness is entirely arbitrary, determined more by the hidden agenda of the person who decides the stage rather than by any objective facts.

The moment of conception (as option 1 above) is the only point at which one can reliably and consistently mark the beginning of a human being. All that is yet to be is potentially present there. What happens thereafter is the realisation of that potential.

We know that the moment the ovum is fertilised by the penetration of the sperm, the twenty-three pairs of chromosomes are complete, the zygote has a unique genotype which is distinct from both parents, and the child's sex, size and shape, colour of skin, hair and eyes, temperament and intelligence are already determined. Each human being begins as a single fertilised cell, while an adult has about thirty million cells. Between these two points (fusion and maturity) forty-five generations of cell division are necessary, and forty-one of them occur before birth.[19]

Humanness from conception is wholly consistent, indeed necessary to, a Christian view of life and the doctrine of man. It is implicit in the Bible, notably in Psalm 139, and most vividly demonstrated in the incarnation of Christ. It has been taught by the church from its earliest days. Let the Reformer, John Calvin, be its spokesman:

The fetus, though enclosed in the womb of its mother, is already a human being, and it is a most monstrous crime to rob it of the life which it has not yet begun to enjoy. If it seems more horrible to kill a man in his own house than in a field, because a man's house is his place of most secure refuge, it ought surely to be deemed more atrocious to destroy the fetus in the womb before it has come to light.[20]

That position has been widely held to in the church until recent times, often against the pressure of the culture with which it was surrounded, believing it to be essential to humane civilisation.

Reverence for human life is an indispensable characteristic of a humane and civilised society.[21]

Surely, someone will say, it's different if the baby is handicapped. Well, is it? That every couple wants a perfect baby is accepted. Very few have one! Of course, in most cases any deformity or disability is slight and it may be years before it is apparent. A bent finger, a cockled ear, short-sightedness—there are so many possibilities. We would actually find it harder to explain what we meant by 'perfect'. But at some point minor imperfections cease to be minor. Who is to say when that point is reached? What if one leg is shorter than another; how great must be the difference? Is a squint acceptable in one eye; what if it is in both?

You must forgive me if I seem pedantic, but this is such an important issue. If we say that handicapped babies should be eliminated, we must decide whether we mean all handicaps or only some. If only some, then where is the line drawn—and by whom? Try it for yourself. Suppose a baby is born with a toe missing, is that OK? If so, suppose it has a foot missing? Is that OK? If so, suppose it has a deformed leg which ends at the knee? Should it be destroyed for want of half a leg? Do you see the point?

In respect of Down's syndrome the medical profession is

quite clear. As it is possible to tell whether the baby in the womb has this condition, it can be aborted with a fair degree of certainty that it has a disability. But no one can know how great will be that disability. It is true that some people with Down's syndrome are very seriously limited in their abilities. It is equally true that some can drive, work, and participate in community life fully.

> Maurice Baring used to tell the story of one doctor who asked another: 'About the termination of pregnancy, I want your opinion. The father was syphilitic, the mother tuberculous. Of the four children born the first was blind, the second died, the third was deaf and dumb and the fourth was tuberculous. What would you have done?' 'I would have ended the pregnancy.' 'Then you would have murdered Beethoven.'[22]

Parliament has opened a can of worms by assenting to the abortion of handicapped babies up to birth. The focus of research may now turn to 'search and destroy' operations. It creates moral dilemmas for doctors in that there is a line to be crossed, a decision to be made. If we accept that no baby should be killed in the womb, that every reasonable effort should be made to maintain life, then we remove the dilemma. And we eliminate the possibility that at some time in the future the parent of a handicapped person will be rudely affronted with the question, 'Why did you allow it to live?'

Why should the baby not live? If capable of being born, why should he or she be so devalued as to be destroyed in the womb? Even if the child will only live a few days, why should not those days be enriched with loving care? If the baby survives and lives, why should not the community into which it is born treat the child with dignity and provide the needed support through its few or many years?

The extent of the child's suffering will be largely determined by the attitudes of those about it. It is not uncommon to hear handicapped people referred to, demeaningly, as 'vegetables'. Indeed one wonders whether Parliament was sufficiently thoughtful of the message they would send to every person with a handicap when they marked them out for particularly destructive mention. It was as if they were saying, 'We don't want any more like you,' to all disabled people. Expressed like that, the inhumanity of what they agreed to beggars belief.

> One striking aspect of this debate is that it has taken place with so little consideration for the feelings and position of the handicapped people who are actually living their lives. We can only speculate what effect the admissibility and legitimation of infanticide has on those directly concerned, what a threat it must be to the self-esteem and self-confidence of handicapped people. The debate articulates and makes respectable the lesser social value that is indeed put on the lives of mentally handicapped people by the way we treat them. It sanctions the expression of rejecting and intolerant attitudes in a dangerous and harmful form. It once again makes the handicapped person into the problem, rather than our own responses, attitudes and resources.[23]

News of Parliament's decision to allow abortion for handicapped babies up to birth came through during the last week of Spring Harvest in 1990. During the evening celebration there was a moving moment for the thousands present. All those who had a disability or handicap were asked either to stand themselves or for someone to stand on their behalf. Scores rose to their feet. From the platform, on behalf of the whole congregation, those present with disabilities were affirmed and their value declared. They were prayed for that they would have courage to bear the stigma placed on them by the government of the day. Would that such affirmation could be expressed from time to time in every church in the land!

Again we have to return to what we are and the value we have as human beings. Any decision to end the life of another person effectively denies that 'every human being has an inalienable dignity just in virtue of his or her humanity.'[24]

We have yet to raise as a defence of vulnerable people arguments which show the sanctity of life. The notion of inviolable life is helpful since, unlike the term 'sanctity', it has no religious connotations and may therefore appeal to those who lack religious convictions. It is built into the United Nations Declaration of Human Rights which says, in Article 3: 'Everyone has the right to life, liberty and security of person.'

> In fact the question is not whether human life is inviolable, but whether we want it to be inviolable. If we want our lives to be protected by the law, then we must decide that human life is inviolable, which means that each human life is inviolable and that it is never permissible to end the life of a human being. . . . Either human life is inviolable, or it is destructible. We can't have it both ways. If we make one exception, where deliberate killing is called good to solve a problem, then human life is no longer inviolable but has become destructible instead. If we decide that human life is inviolable, then everybody's life must be protected by law.[25]

Perhaps the most common argument in favour of abortion, infanticide and euthanasia relates to 'quality of life' considerations. What it suggests is that everyone should have the opportunity to live a life worth living. Few would argue with that. Indeed it provides significant motivation to ensure that this is within everyone's grasp. But it raises a question as to whether some people are incapable of achieving a worthwhile life.

A German philosopher, Hegel, popularised the idea that 'what is useful is good'. An extension of his view was that there could be a life which is not worthy to be lived. That is what is being said today of people with mental handicaps and is resulting in the death of thousands of them, mostly before they are even born. And it is not the first time this has happened in European history. It was that same philosophy which provided a rationale for some of the horrors perpetrated under Hitler. This is how a member of staff in a home for mentally handicapped children explained what happened in her experience:

> One day we heard that the government was planning to take them [the children] away to kill them, just because they were

retarded or handicapped. At first we could not believe this, but we prayed anyway. Oh, how we prayed for our children! But one day the vans came and soldiers took away our little babies. They threw them into the vans like sacks of potatoes and took them off to the 'killing centres'. They said they were killed because they couldn't make a contribution to the Third Reich. They were only an expense, a burden.[26]

John Powell, who reports this incident in *Abortion: the Silent Holocaust*, goes on to say:

At least a quarter of a million Gentile lives were taken because they were deemed 'not meaningful or productive'. With all this blood on his hands, Hitler felt empowered to announce: 'And now we must undertake the final solution of the Jewish problem'.[27]

I do not intend to be alarmist by making this connection, but he who does not learn the lessons of history is in danger of learning nothing!

What do we mean when we speak of 'quality of life'? It is a question preoccupying social services departments who draw up criteria by which to assess the quality of life in residential care homes which they have to oversee. The task is far from easy. It is not difficult to assess whether a house has enough rooms, is warm and light, has tasteful decor and sufficient staff. Quality is actually about less tangible things which are difficult to measure or tick on a checklist. It is concerned with 'atmosphere', relationships between residents and staff, and between residents and residents. Some years ago Madeleine and I visited a home for adults with mental handicaps. On the way home Madeleine commented that she didn't see anyone smile while we were there.

Alison Davis described herself as a 'happy spina bifida adult' who uses a wheelchair. She is convinced that:

'Most handicapped people are quite contented with the quality of their lives'. After all, it is love which gives quality to life and makes it worth living, and it is we—their neighbours—who can choose whether to give love to the handicapped or withhold it. The quality of their life is in our hands.[28]

Writing in 1981, the late Malcolm Muggeridge expressed himself strongly in *The Sunday Times*:

It requires no great prophetic power to foresee that the trial and acquittal of Dr Arthur may likewise be expected to prepare the way for acceptance of euthanasia as part of our contemporary way of life. At first it will be a matter of disposing of seriously handicapped children who, for whatever reason, may be plausibly regarded as unlikely to appreciate the full quality of life today— that is to say, to travel, drive a motor car, have sex, watch television, and otherwise relish the devices and desires on offer in the twentieth century.[29]

I find it hard to overstate how important it is that we withstand this 'quality of life' ethic. It is a treacherous deception which robs people of their essential worth and, potentially, of their life.

The value of the person is judged to be relative to the predicted quality of his or her life.[30]

Thus the advocates of this view slide towards deciding whether the person has worth on the grounds of what others think their future quality of life might be!

Don't misunderstand me. We will do everything within our power to ensure that everyone affected by a handicap or disability will enjoy the best and most satisfying life possible, and do so within a community which cares for and respects them. But we must reject the notion that any person or system is free to determine what is an acceptable quality of life, below which any other person might forfeit his or her existence. When I see the benefits to society and individuals of the presence of people with handicaps I tremble to think how impoverished we would be without them.

I try to imagine a world created by the logical extension of this quality of life ethic. It is a world that will answer to no challenges, will abide no struggle, and will tolerate no one unless his life and contribution to society are considered meaningful and worthwhile. It is a world completely streamlined so that we who are fit and productive, as long as we remain so, can soar through it with the maximum amount of pleasure and a minimum amount of pain. In this world there are no calls to human, interpersonal greatness.[31]

We have come to a pretty pass when we argue it is better to be dead than to be handicapped, when we call on our doctors to take life rather than save it.

In the final analysis the spotlight shines on those of us who consider ourselves not handicapped, as having the right and the power to develop such life-and-death policies. And we have to ask ourselves whether we will hold to the equality of life rather than the quality of life.

The moral question for us is not whether the suffering and dying are persons, but whether we are the kind of persons who will care for them without doubting their worth.[32]

And if we will do so, how will our care be expressed?

Notes

[1] J. Vanier, *Man and Woman He Made Them* (Darton, Longman & Todd: London, 1990), p 45.

[2] 'Sterilised at Seventeen', *The Guardian* (18 March 1987).

[3] L. Spriggs, 'Is Reproduction a Right?', *Community Care* (26 April 1990): p 15.

[4] Prof Glanville, quoted by the Duke of Norfolk in the House of Lords, 18 October 1990. See *Hansard*.

[5] R. Senior, *Towards a Better Understanding* (Euromonitor: London, 1985), p 72.

[6] *Ibid.*

[7] *Ibid*, p 74.

[8] E. Koop and F. Schaeffer, *Whatever Happened to the Human Race?* (Marshall, Morgan & Scott: Basingstoke, 1980), p 449.

[9] Quoted by E. Koop, *ibid*, p 126.

[10] *Ibid*, p 55.

[11] E. Younghusband, 'The Right to Die', *Community Care* (29 March 1978): p 16.

[12] J. Fletcher, quoted by E.W. Lusthaus, 'Involuntary Euthanasia and Current Attempts to Define Persons with Mental Retardation as Less Than Human', *Mental Retardation*, vol 23 (June 1985): p 151.

[13] W. Wolfensberger quoted *ibid*.

[14] Nigel de S. Cameron, *Death without Dignity* (Rutherford House: Edinburgh, 1990), p 45.

[15] Lusthaus, *op cit*, p 148.

[16] J. Fletcher, quoted by Lusthaus, *op cit*.

[17] R. Winter, *Choose Life* (Marshall, Morgan & Scott: Basingstoke, 1988), p 15.

[18] *Ibid*.

[19] J. Stott, *Issues Facing Christians Today* (Marshall, Morgan & Scott: Basingstoke, 1984), p 289.

[20] Winter, *op cit*, p 65.

[21] Stott, *op cit*, p 283.

[22] N. St John Stevas, quoted by Stott, *op cit*, p 296.

[23] J. Ryan and F. Thomas, *The Politics of Mental Handicap* (Free Association Press: London, 1991), p 162.

[24] L. Gormally, in *Death without Dignity, op cit*, p 54.

[25] K. Gunning, *ibid*, p 5.

[26] Quoted by J. Powell, *Abortion: the Silent Holocaust* (Argus Communications: USA, 1981), p 26.

[27] *Ibid*, p 57.

[28] Stott, *op cit*, p 295.

[29] Quoted by D.C. Potter, *Too Soon to Die* (Evangelical Press: Welwyn, 1982), p 95.

[30] J.M. Gustafson, quoted by Lusthaus, *op cit*, p 149.

[31] Powell, *op cit*, p 137.

[32] A. Dyck, quoted by E. Koop, in *Death without Dignity, op cit*, p 121.

9
So What?

*All very interesting I'm sure. But not my responsibility;
definitely not my scene!*

You're not serious? Hasn't this book taught you anything?

*Oh yes, I now feel I know a good deal more about mental
handicap, and I'm glad to be more well-informed. But
knowledge is only power if you choose to use it. I am choosing
not to!*

That, I suggest, is not how God sees things. He regards
knowledge as responsibility rather than power. Knowing
should be followed by doing. You remember the parable of
the wise man who built his house on the rock? Jesus
introduced it like this: 'Everyone who hears these words of
mine and puts them into practice is like a wise man who built
his house on the rock' (Mt 7:24). On another occasion he
said, 'Blessed are those who hear the word of God and obey
it' (Lk 11:28). When talking to his disciples just before he
died Jesus said, 'Now that you know these things, you will
be blessed if you do them' (Jn 13:17). James, the brother of
Jesus, wrote to Christian friends like this: 'Do not merely
listen to the word. . . . Do what it says' (Jas 1:22). Not that
I am implying that what I have written is on a par with the
Bible; but it does suggest that there is good to be done.
'Anyone, then, who knows the good he ought to do and
doesn't do it, sins' (Jas 4:17). What you know places you
under an obligation to do something.

Ah, yes, but this is an issue for experts.

That is only partly true. If only experts were to respond, most of the needs of people with mental handicaps would go unmet because there are relatively few specialists in the field. Many of the issues facing families and individuals where there is a mental handicap are really quite ordinary, like going shopping or finding transport for a hospital visit. What is needed most of all is friendship—something everyone can give and receive.

You *can* make a difference! The problem may seem to you to be immense, affecting more people than you will meet in a lifetime, requiring more skill than you could acquire in years. But the contribution you can make has the potential to transform the lives of individuals. The story is told of an old man walking along a beach which stretched for miles somewhere in South Africa. Thousands of sea creatures had been left behind by the ebb tide, and as he walked the old man would pick up and throw back into the sea some of the small shells. A young passer-by mocked him, 'Hey, old man, what difference do you think that will make? There are thousands more you will never save.' 'True,' replied the old man. 'But for every one I throw back into the waves it is the difference between life and death.'

We Christians could be ahead of everyone else in encouraging people with mental handicaps, supporting their families and doing all we can to integrate them into the body of Christ. We have seen in earlier chapters that this is not the case. It is time to reflect on how we, in our time and generation, will translate what we know into responsible activity.

The difference of friendship

I remember an old lady, blind and bedridden, who lived near a home for people with mental handicaps. She wanted so much to help them but felt quite unable to do so. When she died there were among the mourners some of the residents from the nearby home. She had enriched their lives by welcoming their visits and valuing their friendship.

Being available is at the heart of a Christian response.

Let's listen to Jesus' parable of that extraordinary man, the good Samaritan. This Samaritan had an extremely sensitive heart, and when he saw the assaulted traveller lying on the roadside, he asked himself: 'What will happen to him if I don't stop?' The priest and the Levite, on the other hand, asked themselves: 'What will happen to me if I stop?' The wrong question.[1]

Did you note the focus of the questions? If we are concerned first for ourselves then we will be aware of our vulnerability. 'What if I can't cope?' 'What if I don't understand what he says?' 'Will she be aggressive?'—and so on. Just as the Samaritan might have wondered whether he risked being attacked and left for dead alongside the man he wanted to help. Maybe he should hurry on and call the experts to deal with the situation. (Thank goodness for the Jericho police force!)

Just imagine what would not have happened if God had taken towards us the attitude that we often adopt towards people in need. His Son would almost certainly never have been born and definitely would not have been executed as a punishment for our sins. His objective could only be achieved by becoming involved and thus becoming vulnerable. It was the ultimate expression of friendship, to create friendship. Jesus put it like this:

Greater love has no-one than this, that he lay down his life for his friends. You are my friends if you do what I command. I no longer call you servants. . . . Instead, I have called you friends (Jn 15:13–15).

Friends accept one another as equals, as those with whom they can relax, be honest and just be themselves. Within this relationship it is easy to observe the Golden Rule: 'Do to others as you would have them do to you' (Lk 6:31). Respect and support flow in both directions between friends—and those who befriend people with mental handicaps and their carers will find that this flow is in no way diminished.

You won't have to look far to find people with mental handicaps. The majority of them are already living in the community, at home with their families. Those who are still children will usually attend a special school, travelling to and fro by coach, minibus or taxi. Over-nineteen-years-of-age adults with a mental handicap usually attend a day centre of some sort, as a rule travelling by special transport. Occasionally you may meet some using public transport unaccompanied.

Every area has a variety of local organisations providing support for people with mental handicaps and their families. Best known are the parent groups linked to MENCAP. Additionally there are parent support groups specific to particular forms of handicap, like the Down's Syndrome Association and the National Autistic Society. Between them they run various clubs and social events for children and adults, meetings for mutual support, campaigning and sharing information. Such groups are always looking for volunteers to enhance their ability to do more for their members.

Some people with mental handicaps still live in long-stay mental handicap hospitals. These institutions are being phased out and in some areas they have already closed down. The closure programmes should be complete by the end of the century. As long as they exist they challenge Christians to help break down the isolating effect imposed on those who live in them.

Thousands of adults with mental handicaps live in smaller homes in or near the community. Some are run by local authorities, some by health authorities, some by charities and some by individuals or companies as a business. They are extremely diverse. In the 1970s the pattern favoured by local authorities was twenty-four-bed hostels. Some continue in this form. Several charities have specialised in developing village communities in rural settings, providing a total environment for their residents. Increasingly these are spawning small satellite homes in neighbouring towns and villages. Many 'group homes' exist in ordinary houses, usually of the larger variety to provide the extra space needed. This achieves more dispersement in society.

So, if you have no involvement at all and don't know where to begin, there is sure to be something you can do not far from where you are to establish contact with people with mental handicaps and their families. A telephone call to the local social services department, contact with the local Community Mental Handicap Team, a visit to the special school, a letter to a national organisation seeking the address of the local secretary, a drop-in call to a residential care home—in no time you will find yourself in touch with a whole world of activity, interest, need and opportunity. Almost everywhere you will find a welcome.

You may already have some contact. That is the place to start. Perhaps your neighbour has an adult son with a mental handicap still living at home; or a young couple in your church may have learned that their child has a mental handicap; or a Christian friend helps in a voluntary organisation. Start as near as possible to where you are. We Christians are given to fantasise about what great work God might give us to do (we call them visions!) as founder of this or chairman of that; or how we might trust God for thousands of pounds to build or buy or provide. . . . While we dream, people ache for friendship!

Apply the Golden Rule to your response. Imagine that you are a person with a mental handicap. How would you feel if you had lived through twenty or thirty years of being disregarded by the majority of people whom you meet, or facing rejection and hostility from the people you pass in the street? What sort of understanding would you like to receive from other people? Many issues will crop up, and it is time for us to be more specific. Let's try to group them together to help us think about them and how we may respond.

Where it hurts

It all begins in the family. That's where the news breaks with devastating impact. Dreams lie shattered. Fear of the unknown overwhelms. That is the first place to show loving concern and support, even if there has been no prior contact with you or your church. But be patient. When the first trauma is past you may be able to help parents limp towards a positive view of what has happened, but while the news is still fresh the prospect of a baby who is less than perfect will seem only negative.

All research studies have shown an adverse effect on families' physical and psychological health unless practical and emotional sustenance was offered and accepted.[2]

Nowadays it is possible for the news to be broken even before the baby is born. Tests may have shown that the child has a handicapping condition and a 'termination' will be offered, even if the birth is imminent. The thesis of this book is that there is no reason to accept that offer. Even if the condition is known to be severe, as in the case of anencephaly, there is still a human life involved, a person to be respected. At this point the family need more than prohibitions. In the awful loneliness of looking into the future they need people who will understand and support them. They need to know that if they decide not to snuff out the unborn life, or refuse proffered infanticide, you will be there to share the heartache with them; that you will not only have stood by principles but will also bring practical, tangible love and concern.

Christians don't find it easy to accept suffering, as we saw in an earlier chapter. It challenges our view of a loving God, our assumption that we would somehow have a trouble-free existence. (However did we form this impression when the founder of our faith was crucified?) We tend to cope with it by sticking plasters over open wounds—'You are sharing in Christ's sufferings,' we say. 'You must be very special people for God to allow you to suffer like this.' Or perhaps the irrepressible optimism of faith will bounce back saying, 'Perhaps the child will grow out of it,' when it has a life-long condition which cannot be treated.

Platitudes will not help the family. Even the promise that

you will pray for them may bring scant joy. It is your love they will need, love which will weep with those who weep, will touch their despair, and only then stagger forward in faith in God's comfort for those who mourn the loss of hopes and dreams. It is better to face facts than to play games with false hopes.

If you are a parent yourself, with 'normal' healthy children, you should be able to feel yourself into the emotions of someone who has discovered that her first child will be permanently handicapped. Remember what pictures you drew of your child's future, what fun you planned, what games you would play, how your own joy in living would be extended by this young life. Imagine how you might have struggled if you had watched that child fail to learn, to talk, to respond, to develop. You may then imagine how your friend or neighbour longs for someone who will accept her outbursts, feel her frustration and just be there alongside.

Befriending a family with a mentally handicapped child will bring a variety of needs to light and provide numerous opportunities to be of practical assistance. Shopping can be a nightmare with a hyperactive child, or one liable to wander innocently away while mother struggles through the check-out in a busy supermarket. Getting young children to different schools, waiting for the coach on the corner in an icy wind with another child crying in the push-chair because of cold; it is a harrowing experience. Being able to go out for a meal or a concert knowing that the baby-sitter can cope is a rare experience for many families with a handicapped child.

> The idea of that social desert began to haunt us—there were no friends, no invitations—we had for some time been feeling like social pariahs in the neighbourhood—for Kim we began to realise this would be the way she lives her whole life.[3]

There are, of course, many services provided by local and health authorities to assist families in their care of people with mental handicaps. The authorities are not always as responsive as one might hope and, especially for the family with a young child, finding a way through the system can be daunting. Someone from the church who knows the system could provide enormous help in coping with impersonal bureaucracy. Just being accompanied to the clinic or the social services department will prove such a support.

As the years pass circumstances and needs change. By the time the person with a mental handicap is an adult the range of difficulties may be substantially different from those presented in childhood. Suppose, for instance, that the person requires help to bathe, to get in and out of a wheelchair, or to dress. The time will come when parents find themselves less and less able to provide adequate physical care. One or two trusted friends could do so much to ease the burden, not only of providing care but of preventing the parents bewailing their own failure.

When one parent dies the handicapped person may face a new range of issues. A father left to care for a daughter who needs help to cope with periods; a mother unable to take a son to the local football match; the parent left is unable to drive and cannot take the person for the accustomed Sunday afternoon car-ride. In response the person with a handicap may express frustration by aggression towards the parent. It would be so easy to relieve the situation for them. Looking and listening is the key to meaningful support for families.

Let's turn the focus from the family to the individual who happens to be mentally handicapped. Many we will get to know will not be living with Mum and Dad any more. What do we need to do to help them? First and foremost, see that person as an individual. The fact that he attends church as part of a group—'the mentally handicapped'—must not mask the fact that each one is a unique person to be appreciated and valued in his or her own right.

In most churches there will be one or two people who are prepared to get stuck in and make person to person contact with people attending from a local residential care home. And the rest of the congregation may hide behind them! 'Oh, those are Mrs White's people.' Why shouldn't Mr Brown and Miss Green also get involved so that each one may be befriended?

Children with a mental handicap may be ignored while brothers and sisters receive attention. Staring past them at their relatives will make them feel unwanted. Recognising individuals is an essential precursor to integration. It is very difficult to integrate a category or group of little known people. It is much less difficult to involve Mary because we know her personally. We understand that she becomes anxious in strange situations. We know she can chatter uncontrollably when excited. And we can thus anticipate how to help her so that she, and we, cope satisfactorily. So long as we remain isolated from people with mental handicaps so long will we find it difficult to think of them as equals, and so long will it be hard to imagine them as part of our community or church life. But once we experience the warmth of their friendship we will more readily see their positive qualities than think of them in negative terms—less able, less articulate, less socially competent, and so on.

Friendship will aid increased independence, if only because friends draw on each other. Inviting a person home for coffee or a meal on his own will give a great sense of being significant. For some it may prove a unique experience! Taking a teenage girl with a mental handicap to a fashion show, or a child to the circus, will be a thoroughly memorable experience. Such outings will need preparation; contact with carers will alert you to anything which might prove awkward. For example, taking a person to the cinema may have to be abandoned because he refuses to enter the auditorium for fear of the dark.

Helping a person learn to use public transport rather than taking him by car may prove a real step forward to regular use of buses or trains. It will then require sustained training over weeks and months, with diminishing levels of support. Again the agreement and help of carers is essential; the risks are real; the gains are enormous. In due course the person may be able to get himself to church on his own, or attend the day centre without having to use the minibus.

Being an advocate for our friends is something which comes naturally to us. If we hear them being run down we take their part and speak up for them. We may find that the parents we befriend need our advocacy in dealing with the education department or the school or the social services department. If we feel ill-equipped for the task we may persuade the pastor or some Christian friend to get involved. The mentally handicapped person living in a residential home may feel crushed by a member of staff and need someone to speak to the manager responsible so that the difficulty can be ironed out. Again, it's a matter of putting ourselves in the other person's shoes.

Out there in the community the main obstacles, as we have seen, are fear and prejudice. Both are based on ignorance and 'folklore'. For those who do not know people with mental handicaps it is not difficult to believe the popular myths about them. This breeds hostility and misunderstanding. Unreasonable expectations are placed on people with mental handicaps which would not be accepted by most non-handicapped people. A Cause for Concern received a strongly worded protest letter about its home for two people. It ran to two pages and dripped with venom! At the end of the letter I thought how fortunate our neighbours were that the house we had bought was not occupied by a family with teenage children. Their radios and motor bikes might have caused far more disruption—but that would have been seen as 'normal'.

This sort of prejudice does not yield to rational debate. It only gives way to real experience which shows things as they really are. That is where you and I come in. We can push back the barriers of ignorance by speaking of known people. When they trot out the fables and horror stories we can tell them about John and Mark and Susan. When there was vigorous opposition to a new home for people with mental handicaps in Bayston Hill the local church arranged for the protesters to visit a home in Aberystwyth run by the same charity. Most declined, but those who accepted the invitation dropped their opposition.

The church can provide a welcoming model for the community in respect of local people who have a mental handicap. Members may first have to overcome their own fear and learn to cope with difficulties created by a visiting group who are unwittingly disruptive of the quiet order of Sunday morning. The congregation at St Michael's became very concerned about the attendance of four men from the newly opened residential care home. They talked during prayers, moved around the church during the hymns and, most embarrassingly, answered the preacher's rhetorical questions during the sermon! For the sake of everyone, something had to be done. One option was to ask them not to come any more. As one member said, 'We are not usually keen to *stop* people coming to church!'

Instead they devised another approach. Four families agreed to befriend one of the group each. After the next service each family chatted with one of the men and before saying goodbye invited him to sit with them the following Sunday. A friendship developed which spilled over from Sunday morning to an invitation to Sunday lunch, to exchanging birthday cards, sharing picnics, and so on. It took time, but proved a real boon. Within the security of the friendship the tendency of one of the men to talk during prayers could be corrected. By example and advice all four learned a greater degree of conformity. But also the church discovered a new level of informality entering its worship.

So long as some people with mental handicaps remain in institutions the local church must not lose sight of their needs. The issues will be different. There may well be some hundreds of people living together, sharing their space with several others in large wards, separated from the next person by only a curtain or wardrobe. The patients, or residents, live an orchestrated life where they are able to make very few choices, share clothes and toothbrushes (yes, it is still happening), having little privacy and even less hope. While most hospitals do have a chaplain, there is still much that can be done to provide Christian input, which is sure to be welcomed by the chaplain. When eventually the local hospital does close the local church can provide caring support for what is inevitably a traumatic move. It requires not so much professional skill, but love for people who are not always obviously lovable. You will be touching pain as you bring healing to wounded spirits, and that you cannot do without feeling pain yourself. But in due course you will share in the joy that will follow.

Dennis had to live for a while in a mental handicap hospital because his behaviour was such his parents could not cope. After some time he improved and returned home, though he still used the hospital day centre. Some Christians welcomed Dennis at the local church, and through that contact he began to attend a Bible group for people with mental handicaps. His confidence grew with the wider contact with people. After a year or two Dennis was converted, and his parents noticed a difference in his behaviour and attitudes. Later he asked to be baptised—the family was there to share the occasion. When asked why he wanted to be baptised Dennis replied, 'Jesus is the best friend I've ever had!' Some time later still Dennis stood up to share some news with his friends in the Bible group. 'The hospital has said they don't want me any more. I'm too good for them.' Professionals had agreed that he had made so much improvement that he no longer needed their supervision. The members of the group cheered the news. The leaders beamed!

Where there is need

Book titles can be fascinating. One I saw recently was *All you love is need*. It's thought-provoking, isn't it. People who serve on committees with social services departments or health authorities will find it strikes a chord. There seems no shortage of statistics to inform their deliberations; need can be quantified and stratified endlessly. But sometimes, I fear, that is all that is achieved. People barely feature in the discussion.

The needs we see around us are of enormous diversity and weight. It is small wonder that people become immune to the pressure of them. At church level there are far more needs within the community than any congregation can hope to meet. However, our focus and our calling are not to needs but to people. God sees the tears and pain and fears and hopes of people. He hears their despairing cries. And it is through his own people that he wishes to make his response tangible. We have seen that historically the church has been less than sensitive to the heartbeat of God for people with mental handicaps. We are challenged to respond differently from our forebears. So that we may better identify ways in which we can achieve this we will focus on some aspects of life where people with handicaps are at a disadvantage.

For want of a job

Most readers of this book will be in some form of employment, even if that is in the home. The fact that unemployment figures are headline news reflects the general expectation of a meaningful and rewarding career. However, the prospect of a career is unlikely to be very great for a person who has a mental handicap. The main daytime activity for such a person, regardless of his ability, is likely to be in a day centre of some description.

Day services face critical difficulties, made the more so because of the numbers of people who have moved out of long-stay hospitals into community placements. County after county reports the same pattern—too few places at Adult Training Centres (ATCs) or Social Education Centres (SECs) as they are variously known. Managers of centres are ingenious at maximising their resources, organising attendance at colleges of further education, swimming and horse riding. Even so there are limits on what they can achieve and the numbers they can co-ordinate in this way. Increasingly families are finding that at nineteen their son or daughter is offered only a part-time placement at the day centre.

It is not only very normal to want a career, it is

fundamentally human too! It is a consequence of being made in God's image. Creativity is derived from the Creator.

> There is need for a proper philosophy of work which understands work not as that which it has indeed become, an inhuman chore as soon as possible to be abolished by automation, but as something decreed by Providence for the good of man's body and soul.[4]

The notion of employment for people with mental handicaps is hardly mentioned, yet it could go a long way to easing the pressure on slender local authority resources. Let me quote, at length, from someone who is expert in this field and who knows from experience what possibilities there are.

> Contrary to the general belief of both public and professionals, many people with learning difficulties have the potential to successfully obtain full or part-time, open or sheltered, socially valued and unsegregated employment. There are thousands of people with a mental handicap around the country who have been successful in their search for employment. Placements have been secured in a variety of work settings, including offices, hotels, catering establishments and supermarkets. . . . The rewards from employment are immense, and in some cases immeasurable. . . . Having a job increases self-esteem, confidence and individuality; the opportunity to work alongside other people increases social awareness and, more importantly, social relationships. Work develops the opportunity for integration into, and acceptance by, society itself; the employed person becomes part of our consumer society, and through experience they become less dependent on their families and the community and can therefore take advantage of the social opportunities that surround them. Employment provides a new and exciting dimension to their lives.[5]

Jean Vanier found that work helped personal development for people in L'Arche.

> There was an unmistakable happiness that sprang from a handicapped person's discovery that he or she could make something beautiful or useful.[6]

What a pity that so much potential is held back. People
with mental handicaps have frequently shown themselves to
be reliable and competent employees. The majority do not
have the opportunity to prove themselves able to work.
Government policy on benefits is also partly to blame. Above
a modest figure, any earnings on the part of the person with
a mental handicap will result in the loss of state benefits.
Such people are then caught in a poverty trap, unable to earn
sufficient to pay their way in a residential care home, but
losing the benefits that are needed if they are paid more than
a nominal wage. Yet if those benefits were reduced pro rata
they would be able to enjoy the freedom and dignity of
working, and be in a position to pay their fees. At the same
time places would be released in ATCs, allowing those unable
to cope with employment to continue receiving a full-time
day service.

There are jobs which can be done by people with relatively
limited ability in all sorts of work settings. Residents in homes
run by A Cause for Concern work part-time in a bakery, a
mother and toddler group, a shop, a garage, a supermarket,
a printing factory, as domestics, and so on. One man holds
down a full-time job as a kitchen porter. Another works in
an office photocopying and assembling information packs.

Employers must be willing to offer the jobs. If they
will have imagination in this respect they will expand the
horizons of people with mental handicaps considerably.
These employees may need more training, a supporting
person during the first few weeks, a longer trial period. But
given sympathetic help the potential for developing successful
and committed employees is considerable.

Other employees must be persuaded to co-operate in the
venture. Some will react negatively because of their fears of
people with mental handicaps. The greater danger is that
after the first aversion to the person, other workers will
become protective and patronising so that the handicapped
person does not develop as much as might be possible.

Christians in key positions can help this sort of thing to

happen. They can initiate such schemes in their workplace; they can provide volunteer support; they can arrange transport to and from the workplace. They can even consider setting up a day service in otherwise empty church halls. By such means they can fulfil the dreams of many and help forward the slow process of integration.

Nor does one have to think in terms of large and expensive projects with complex management or potentially dangerous machinery. With imagination, innovative work schemes could be devised for small groups of people with and without disabilities. Smallness has much in its favour, providing opportunity for labour-intensive work in an environment of supportive relationships.

For want of an interest

Just as most of us want a job, so most of us want more leisure time! Evenings and weekends seem too short for all the things we want to do—as well as going to church. The only other bar on doing the things we want to do is usually money—hobbies can be expensive. For the person with a mental handicap there are additional obstacles to overcome.

The first is inertia! Television is the friend of carers, whether family or professional. What is seen on TV may not always be understood or, generally, be beneficial, but many people with mental handicaps spend disproportionately long periods of time in front of its flickering screen. And if one is 'happy' (which probably is assumed to be the case if no complaint is expressed) then why should the person or their carer be concerned?

The second is the fact that most potential leisure pursuits open to people with mental handicaps tend to be social events for others who share their disabilities. So they continue in segregated settings rather than become part of the social life of the community.

The third might be the difficulty of taking the initiative. It is not only that the person may not be able to think of something to do, and with his more limited experience of life this is quite likely, but that he can't use the telephone or public transport or whatever. Or he may never have been taught to make a rug or helped to paint a model aircraft.

Here too there is enormous potential for volunteers to help in transforming the life experience of a person with mental handicaps while enriching their own! Taking a child swimming, playing on the swings on a Saturday afternoon, taking a person out for a meal or to a meeting in someone's home, accompanying him to an evening class, or just having him home for coffee and a game—the possibilities are endless. Becoming involved with people as friends will surely result in sharing our leisure. It is so natural that this should be the case.

For want of understanding

Helping with work and leisure can involve people whether or not they have faith. There is, however, one area of life where the contribution required can only be made by Christians and churches. Indeed if help is not forthcoming from them it will not be available from anyone! It is in the area of spiritual needs that the unique contribution of Christians must also be made.

Jesus wants and expects his followers to evangelise all sorts of people. The good news is for everybody. What is more, the implication of the gospel stories is that those who are regarded as 'outcasts' in society should have a prior place in our concern and outreach. You will recall that Jesus told a parable which allowed the rich to decline an invitation to a banquet, but urged the servants to persuade, even compel, society's outsiders to come in. So people with mental handicaps seem ideal candidates since they have, by and large, been pushed to the fringes of society for so long. But the fact is that they are under-represented in the congregations of all denominations and church groupings. And you will find that evangelistic organisations have a special focus on all sorts of people—young, unemployed, elderly, women, mothers, servicemen, homeless, and so on—but almost never is there a mention of people with mental handicaps. Contrast this with the commission given to us by Jesus. He was adamant that we should spread the good news everywhere, to everybody. When he said we were to go into all the world and make disciples it is clear that he was keen for people of all cultures and languages and tribal groups to know about his love. No one is to be excluded from our evangelism.

We have to establish why people with mental handicaps require attention and what their particular needs are.

The first problem facing a person with a mental handicap is that of getting to church. By expressing the problem in this way we have already assumed that he knows what church is and why he should want to get there, which begs several questions! The problem of 'access' may begin at home. If he cannot speak clearly it may be difficult for the person to express a desire to attend church. If his carer, be that a parent or member of staff, has no wish to attend, his choice is unlikely to be honoured. If the person is able to get out and about by himself but does not know where church is then he cannot readily fulfil his own desire. And perhaps, when his carer will take him, they reach the building only to discover an impossible flight of steps confronting the wheel-chair, if he also has a physical disability.

If that person and you don't know about each other then the likelihood is that he may never get to find out the good news being spoken about each Sunday in your church. Evangelism starts at an earlier stage—and may need wheels to make it effective!

Let's assume that the person has overcome that first problem. He makes it to church next Sunday morning and receives a welcoming hand-shake at the door. (It is not unknown for a handicapped person to be asked to leave at this point.) What else is he likely to be given? Yes, a book. Or even a pile of books—hymn book, Bible, prayer book, song book. We are pleased to be called 'people of the Book' so it is no wonder if the book culture runs deep in our churches. What a good thing it is that God has said what we need to hear, and arranged for it to be written down so that we would not forget. But it assumes an ability to read, and if you can't . . .? At the point of welcome the person with a mental handicap may be reminded of failure. There is potential to embarrass and, unintentionally, to wound.

The third problem to mention is that of concentration span. It is said that a person of average intelligence is able to sustain unbroken attention for a maximum of twenty minutes. Most of the average church service comes in sections—some time for prayer, some for Bible reading, some for singing, and so on. The sermon is likely to be the longest single and sustained part of the service, lasting anything from ten minutes to an hour—depending on what sort of church (or minister) it is. So for most people most of what happens is within range, even if the sermon is followed piecemeal. Suppose, however, that one's concentration span lasts only three or four minutes! It will tend to make all but the briefest parts of the service relatively meaningless. That is the sort of issue facing a person with a mental handicap.

Then there is the content of the service. A high level of attention is on the abstract, expressed in conceptual and theoretical terms. Add to that the extensive use made of metaphor and parable. Mental handicap affects a person's ability to think in anything other than 'concrete' terms. What is seen can be explained and appreciated; what is unseeable is exceedingly difficult to explain so that it can be grasped. It is at this point that one finds comparisons with ministry to children become unhelpful. For example, one might speak to a child about prayer being like talking to God on a telephone. If the child takes it literally he will soon grow up sufficiently to realise that one was using picture language. Such an illustration used with a person with a mental handicap might become fixed as literal, and prove unhelpful since it implies the possibility of God being unavailable to hear our prayers—line engaged!

These obstacles to meaningful attendance at and appreciation of church services result in a low level of church attendance by people with mental handicaps. Clearly this is something which needs to be addressed if they are to be informed of God's love for them, brought to believe in Jesus and made participating members of the body of Christ. And it will require us to be proactive in going where they are and making this good news real and understandable to them.

Hold it! Are we going too far too fast? We are taking it for granted that people with mental handicaps *need* to be evangelised. There are many who will argue that this is not the case. They will say that people with mental handicaps are innocent and do not need to become Christians. They are already accepted by God as they are. It must be admitted that, when faced with a person with a profound degree of handicap, one is perplexed at how to grapple with moral and spiritual issues so as to be relevant and meaningful to that person. In such a situation one acknowledges, for one's self, the desirability of a doctrine of innocence. It would deliver one from the demands of reaching the heart of what we believe and communicating it in some real way to the handicapped person.

However, the Bible simply does not recognise a category of people who are innocent. It states plainly and repeatedly that 'all have sinned'. Even if we argue that sin must be related to knowledge—a view the Bible proposes—the fact of universal sin remains inescapable. Experience confirms that what the Bible says of our sinfulness is true even of people with profound handicaps. Furthermore, the argument of innocence does not remove a problem; it simply moves it. It becomes necessary to discover at what point the degree of handicap does not result in moral innocence. Where are we to draw the line and on what criteria? Which people do we evangelise? A mistake at this point may lead to wasting our time or leaving some hopeless of finding God's peace. If only for safety's sake we would have to exclude none from our concern!

There is an opposite objection to evangelising people with mental handicaps. It is said that they cannot understand sufficient to be saved. Without doubt, the gospel is profound to a degree that exercises the greatest minds. Who can fathom the mystery of God, or grasp the wonder of the Trinity; who can explain why 'God so loved the world that he gave his one and only Son, that whoever believes in him shall not perish but have eternal life' (Jn 3:16)?

We must also admit to over-intellectualising the good news, for there is about it something which is incredibly simple. It is within the range of a child as well. Jesus was actually pleased that it is like this:

> I praise you, Father, Lord of heaven and earth, because you have hidden these things from the wise and learned, and revealed them to little children. Yes, Father, for this was your good pleasure (Mt 11:25–26).

Note the words 'hidden from' and 'revealed to'. Becoming a Christian is not a matter of understanding and assenting to dogma. It is being 'born from above' into a relationship with God; it is a revealed religion, revealed to the heart of a person by the activity of God the Holy Spirit. The theological term is 'regeneration'. A child is more likely to experience that 'revealing' than is a wise person! And, by natural extension we could argue, so is a person with a mental handicap. The cleverest Christian must say, 'It is by grace [we] have been saved, through faith . . .' (Eph 2:8). The person with a mental handicap is familiar with faith since he has to live much of his life dependent on others. Having faith is within his capacity and life experience!

> No matter how complicated, educated, or sophisticated we may be, or how simple we may be, we must all come the same way, in so far as becoming a Christian is concerned. As kings of the earth and the mighty of the earth are born in exactly the same way physically as the simplest man, so the most intellectual person or the most complicated person must become a Christian in exactly the same way as the simplest person.[7]

Our task in evangelism is quite clear from the New Testament: 'God gave us the work of bringing people into peace with him' (2 Cor 5:18, ETRV[8]). This fits with the needs and the potential of people with mental handicaps. It would appear, then, that we have a job to do in which we may expect to have some success. What next?

Start by looking at what you are doing. Here is an exercise for you next time you go to church. Imagine, as best you can, that you have a mental handicap. Note anything you might find difficult, unhelpful, irrelevant or even offensive, from the moment you enter the building until you leave. Then consider how you would help a friend with a mental handicap cope with the problems you met and how you might persuade the church to address the difficulties which they cause. Having done that you will be able to consider more realistically what you should do to reach people with mental handicaps. (Make this a pen-and-paper exercise next Sunday evening.)

The next step is to review existing contact with people with mental handicaps. Is there a family in the church with a mentally handicapped child? How is the child provided for within the life of the church, in Sunday school, youth activities, and so on? You may not be able to do much for one child but that one can be the means of contact with others. Draw the family into discussion about other children at the special school. How can you integrate the child and his friends? How can you meet their particular needs?

There may be an adult with a mental handicap attending the services. How are his spiritual needs being met? Again, this person can provide a wider range of contacts, or parents may offer a link with a local society. In the event of a group of people with mental handicaps attending the services, you may need to ask how relevant church is proving for them. Are they finding friendship? Is their limited life experience taken into account in the worship, the prayers, the ministry? Could the preacher sometimes draw illustration from their lives? Could the sermon include a simple summary of the message so that they could at least grasp the kernel of truth being explained? Could visual aids be used to stretch their concentration span? Almost anything done to enhance the value of the service to people with mental handicaps will also help other members of the congregation.

Church is a desirable activity for people with mental handicaps but it will probably need to be supplemented in ways that relate truth more directly to their life and needs. A meeting for them on a regular basis, say twice monthly, will supplement and make more meaningful their attendance at Sunday services. As it is likely that the numbers of people with mental handicaps attending any given church may be limited, such a meeting could serve folk from a number of local churches. How to go about setting up such meetings has already been explained in detail in *We're All Special to God* by Madeleine and me. The book (published by Scripture Union) goes into detail as to how to lead meetings and provides lesson material as well.

When people with mental handicaps become Christians they will need to be 'discipled' just like anyone else. People need to understand how the Bible relates to their new life and experience, what knowing God means in practice. So people who are new to faith need to be taught. This too can take place in the context of a Bible group for people with mental handicaps. It can be enhanced within a friendship between the new convert and a person without a handicap.

Personal spiritual growth flourishes with regular prayer and Bible reading, both of which express a relationship with God. A person with a mental handicap is faced with quite a challenge in this respect. He may not be able to read, and he may be unused to initiating any private or personal activity such as would be necessary in prayer. The helpful friend can prove invaluable in many ways. He might visit for half an hour two or three times a week to read and explain a short passage from Scripture and to pray together. They might agree to each pray for one person every day, and the friend promise to telephone to help the handicapped person remember. He might provide a card with a verse or two written on it and a short prayer which a carer might be willing to read. There are so many ways which can, with a little imagination and effort, provide enrichment for a person's spiritual life.

So far the traffic has been all one way—from 'us' (who regard ourselves as relatively free of handicaps) to 'them' (the people we regard as handicapped). That is not the whole story by any means!

> Those who know the real joy of sharing a little of the exhilaration of Christian exploration in company with friends who have a mental handicap, will have discovered for themselves the indescribable mutual enrichment which can ensue.[9]

Writing in the mid-70s, Wolfensberger, a leading American exponent of 'normalisation', wrote of his experience in this regard:

> It is only in the last few years that I have been having experiences such as moments of spiritual sharing and worship by groups that may be as large as over a hundred people of whom maybe half are severely retarded and otherwise handicapped, and there may occur striking totality and profundity of silence of a type which overpoweringly conveys the presence of God. . . . One implication of all this is that the retarded people must be related to as partners in the faith.[10]

Which is really what we are urging, a two-way relationship. In giving we receive. What we have proposed so far is not particularly different from the sort of mutual consideration one might look for between Christians, regardless of whether or not they have any handicaps. Nor should it surprise us if a Christian who happens to have a mental handicap makes a spiritual contribution in a service or group meeting. He or she may want to pray for a friend who is ill or to give thanks for someone who has been a help to him or her. That person may not follow the intricacies of a discussion but may be intuitively aware of what is important and speak right to the heart of the issue.

Madeleine and I have benefited so much from the meetings

we have run for people with mental handicaps attending Spring Harvest. Participation is encouraged from the outset and we are frequently amazed at the level and quality of the contributions made. Some will want to lead the meeting in prayer and will do so with a perception of God's love which is deeply moving. Some may share a testimony to what God has done in their lives. Hearing the Bible read by a person with a mental handicap is, for me, one of the most humbling experiences. One woman I know reads in such a way that I look with new eyes at what the passage is saying.

I recall a meeting at which Madeleine spoke about the resurrection of Jesus from the dead. In order to press home the wonderful truth of Easter we handed out small card pictures of the stone which was rolled away from the tomb. Each person was to hand on his or her stone to someone else saying, 'Jesus is alive.' What concern, joy and tenderness was evident as this good news was shared. Many bystanders were overwhelmed by the open sharing that took place.

A similar incident, from the previous year, was recorded by a visitor to a seminar:

The sound of singing drifted towards me from across the passage. I peered through a porthole window in the green door and saw people sitting facing an overhead projector. Someone was playing a guitar. I gently pushed the door open and slid inside, hoping no one would notice me. As I stood at the back of the room, people began to get up and walk around. They were clutching pieces of red paper which I realised were heart shaped.

'Take your heart and give it to someone else in the room. As you give them your heart you are telling them you love them. You are sharing God's love.'

I watched as people slowly rose from their seats and moved towards each other. Suddenly I felt tears running down my face. Why did this scene move me so much? The room was full of mentally handicapped young adults. This was a special seminar at Spring Harvest. . . . I had never been to such a meeting before. There was great warmth and reality in the simple worship. . . . Perhaps the specialness of the Spring Harvest seminar was not that the individuals were handicapped but that other people were at last taking them seriously. Their own simple expression of faith was valued for what it truly was: an act of worship of great value to the God who created them.[11]

Another year at Spring Harvest we had reached the end of our last meeting and were saying farewell. Suddenly a young man took the microphone and told me to sit down. In two minutes he explained the gospel and urged people to believe in the Lord Jesus. Then he handed me back the microphone and sat down. I could hardly speak. The young man, whom I knew well, was mentally handicapped but also had great difficulty in communicating due to a severe impediment of speech. But not this time; there was hardly a moment's hesitation in his impassioned flow of words. I wondered how much we have missed by not allowing the space for him to contribute more often.

We need to ask again the imaginary question of the Good Samaritan: 'What will happen to me if I don't stop?' It is certain that we and our churches will be losers if there are no people with mental handicaps among us, or if, being with us, they are silenced by lack of opportunity to contribute to our life together. As we respond to their needs we shall find that many of our own are met along the way!

Notes

[1] J. Vanier, in *Mental Handicap: Challenge to the Church* (Lisieux Hall: UK, 1991), p 105.

[2] P. Gilbert, *Mental Handicap: A Practical Guide for Social Workers* (Business Press International: UK, 1985), p 46.

[3] M. and D. Collins, quoted in *Mental Handicap: Challenge to the Church, op cit*, p 175.

[4] E.F. Schumacher, *Small is Beautiful* (Abacus: UK, 1974), p 29.

[5] C. Bailey, in Alan Leighton (ed) *Mental Handicap in the Community* (Woodhead-Faulkner: Cambridge, 1991), p 83.

[6] J. Vanier, *A Communion of Love* (Darton, Longman & Todd: London, 1990), p 50.

[7] F. Schaeffer, *True Spirituality* (Hodder & Stoughton: London, 1972), p 15.

[8] The Easy to Read version (ETRV) of the Bible is ideally suited for reading by or with people with a mental handicap. It uses a limited vocabulary but provides footnotes whenever the use of 'special' words is unavoidable, eg disciple, Holy Spirit, etc. Short sentences aid comprehension. Copies are obtainable in the UK only from A Cause for Concern (see p 251 for address). It is available as New Testament only, or a complete Bible in hard or soft cover.

[9] K. Rowlands, in *Mental Handicap: Challenge to the Church*, op cit, p 191.

[10] W. Wolfensberger, *The Prophetic Voice and Presence of Mentally Retarded People in the World Today* (Unpublished paper, 1978), pp 18, 30.

[11] C. Philps, *Mummy, Why Have I Got Down's Syndrome?* (Lion: Oxford, 1991), pp 103, 108.

10

Where There are Difficulties

Quite deliberately I have so far focused on the positive possibilities that exist in befriending people with mental handicaps. You may have found this frustrating because your experience has involved facing many difficulties. So has mine! Working in the field of mental handicap is demanding, but I still want to avoid giving the impression that mental handicap is a 'problem'. It is too often seen as such in society and, regrettably, in the church too. Rather we need to see it as a challenge.

Mental handicap is a challenge to the narrowly defined categories we have adopted from the secular, educationally conditioned, materialistic, success-oriented society in which we live. Those categories confine and constrict the expression of the love of God and the onward march of the body of Christ. Those categories squeeze our compassion, tolerance and fellowship with people who do not fit the criteria of what is popularly admired and acceptable.

> Our ideas of what 'perfect' human beings are, are false and mixed up. They are utilitarian and success oriented. The handicapped often show us what true beauty and true humanity is. . . . If we can let the handicapped challenge our values, something truly creative can happen which can happen in no other way.[1]

This book does not attempt to deny that mental handicap exists. It is a challenge to accept it as part of the normal pattern of life in our churches, to benefit from the added diversity it brings and to overcome the real difficulties it presents to us personally and corporately.

Challenging behaviours

At some stage in our attempts to develop integrated churches 'behaviour' will be an issue. It used to be said that some people with mental handicaps had maladaptive behaviours or behaviour problems. Now they are spoken of as 'challenging behaviours'. The reason for this change in terminology is to shift the focus from the person behaving in a certain way on to our need to understand what it going on. We are all familiar with the idea of 'body language'. For people with limited communication skills this may be the only sort of language they can use effectively. We must return to this issue, but meantime we have to see how this affects church life.

Church has its own particular—even peculiar—culture. Do you know any other meeting of a club, Parent/Teacher Association, political party, or concert where people behave as you do in church? Only in church do we all sing in unison from books or screen; we listen to one person speaking (at some length); notices are given out (by announcement or printed bulletin, or both); sometimes we sit, sometimes stand, and sometimes kneel. Every congregation has its own 'ritual', though some would prefer not to call it that. If you go from one church to another, even within the same denomination, you will find considerable variation on the same theme.

A total stranger to church will need a little time to become familiar with the way things are done. If that person sits in the front row, unable to see what others are doing, it will be more difficult. And if he happens to have a learning disability which prevents him picking up the subtle signals the rest of us observe, then the likelihood is that he will get things wrong and be standing when he should be sitting or singing when he should be praying. Or, in the eyes of some present, he will be misbehaving!

When a person with a mental handicap attends a service for the first time the possibility of disruption is quite high. If accompanied by other, similarly handicapped people, the level of potential disruption is multiplied. Responding to it sensitively and practically is quite a challenge. Difficulties can arise in a number of ways.

Social graces may not have been learned if the person has lived in an institutional environment, with the result that the way that person seeks attention may be blatant. It could be by exhibitionism or by pretending a spiritual response. Aggression is less common than may be feared but there may be occasional grabbing or punching or even biting. A more severely handicapped person may grunt or squeal at inconvenient moments. For a family these forms of behaviour can be acutely embarrassing, the more so if members of the congregation show their disapproval. Even where it has been publicly stated as OK, I have seen parents blush and squirm. If the person with a mental handicap is unaccompanied and no one knows what to do, a paralysis descends on the congregation. Some churches solve the problem by simply saying 'No' to any further attendance. It is a picture which reflects what is happening in the wider society. It is rejection.

What shall we do about it? Exclusion is not an option; indeed, inclusion is mandatory. But however are we to cope with the potential disruption it might cause? As one mentally handicapped friend of mine likes to say, 'Don't panic!' Let's try to understand a little of what is going on. Let's listen to the behaviour.

Some forms of behaviour are fixed in the pattern of a person's life from an early age. These tend to be self-stimulating actions such as rocking to and fro, examining one's own fingers, clucking, twiddling a piece of paper, grinding one's teeth, and so on. They are obsessions which are unlikely to be eliminated. They are often a sign of boredom. Jennie would click her fingers quietly, from silence to a tiny crescendo, as the sermon wore on. I watched the lady in the next row grow tense at this soft intrusion on the silent congregation. She began to throw irritated glances at the person with Jennie. I'm sure she missed the point of the sermon; so did I, but not because of Jennie.

Some things one is less ready to accept. After the service ended Mike would stay sitting in the pew looking sad, or with his head in his hands. Sometimes he would sob quietly. Others who saw him would comfort him and enquire about his tears. They would pray with him as he spoke about the response he wanted to make to the service. But it was a weekly pattern, and people began to doubt his sincerity. Mike was saying something by the way he behaved, but he was misheard. His message was simple: 'I want you to notice me and talk to me.'

Wanting to be noticed, valued and welcomed is a common desire. Most of us achieve this by a variety of subtle strategies. The way we dress, our hair-do, the way we approach other people, are some of them. Mike had fewer options, but he found a way that worked week after week. Sadly it became counter-productive. It was resolved easily enough: he was given attention when he wasn't demanding it! He soon found that mock tears were not required.

Some behaviours say, 'I can't cope,' or 'I don't know what to do.' These may be disruptive expressions of insecurity. One evening Helen stormed out of the house group swearing at her host and his wife. The group was astonished at such a seemingly unprovoked display. The young man leading the meeting for the first time was thoroughly unsettled. Only later was it possible to piece together what had gone wrong. The inexperienced leader had suggested that they each read a verse of the Bible passage they were considering. Helen was under threat; she could not read. Not knowing what to do led to an emotional explosion. She knew no other way of coping.

Almost every form of inappropriate behaviour will be diminished if someone will befriend the individual concerned. Loud singing of the hymns, talking during the prayers, wandering during the sermon, hugging and kissing total strangers—the power of example, spoken advice, a restraining hand on the arm, all given by someone known to value the individual, will soon bring difficult or embarrassing situations under control. At the same time, those quirks and odd actions which do not disrupt or interfere will take their place within the person's routine as part of the congregation.

Children with mental handicaps also tend to challenge the norm. The typical response to their needs tends to increase rather than decrease difficulty. The assumption is made that they should be with children younger than themselves, on the fallacious basis of 'mental age'. It frequently results in situations which are ludicrous—a girl of Guides age remaining in Brownies; a boy in senior school continuing in the infants class at church. They are exposed to ridicule by other children. They are segregated from their peers who could learn to accept and help them. Being with their own age group they may learn less from the theoretical teaching given, but they will be better adapted socially and better able to cope with their handicap.

Bereavement is another issue which requires sensitive consideration, the more so since many adults with a mental handicap carry difficulties resulting from past experience of insensitivity. Nowadays it is likely that most mentally handicapped people will outlive their parents. If this real fact is not handled wisely, both by parents and friends, it can be the cause of long-standing problems.

Jim's mother was ill and his father was finding it difficult to cope with his mentally handicapped son as well as his increasingly dependent wife. So Jim went to stay with his auntie 'for a few days'. She was his favourite so all was fine, until days stretched into weeks and weeks to months. Occasionally his father wrote to him or telephoned. Eventually Jim learned that he would be going home. He was so excited at seeing his father again that he did not understand all that was being said to him as they travelled together. When, at last, he was home again he was confused, angry and terribly sad. His mother was not there. She had gone. Another lady shared his father's room, a lady he used to see at church. Only slowly did he grasp the situation—his mother had died while he was away and his father had married a lady who had helped him nurse her. After that whenever Jim heard about death he went to pieces. Now Jim's father is old and frail, and Jim is worried sick about the future.

It's another true story. For some reason it is thought that people with mental handicaps will not understand about death and dying. Mature people are prevented from attending funerals and discouraged from expressing grief simply because they have a mental handicap. It is a wholly irrational reaction on the part of otherwise rational people. No doubt the motives are good, but the outcome is bad.

No less than others, people with mental handicaps need to be brought into the experience of bereavement, helped to grieve, supported through their sense of loss and given help to cope with the ensuing loneliness. It can happen.

Sheila was living in a home with people who, like herself, had a mental handicap. She was a kind and popular lady loved by residents and staff alike. She became seriously ill and it was evident that she was dying. So it was arranged that she would return to the home from hospital, with additional nursing care being provided. For a few more weeks, as her grip on life loosened, she continued to live among her friends. They would sit quietly by her bed, or pop in for a few minutes to talk to her. When she lost consciousness one or another would stand vigil over her so that she would not feel lonely if she woke up. When she died her friends grieved. They attended the funeral and the committal. They visited her now empty room. In due course they came through their grief and now talk cheerfully about Sheila. They remember her with happiness.

There are two other aspects of behaviour that we need to consider briefly before we move on. First the matter of discipline. Parents of a person with a mental handicap must have the courage to exercise discipline! It is difficult to do in the face of the child's handicap, and it takes a good deal longer. But allowing the child to be spoilt by overindulgence will serve to increase the difficulties she or he will experience on reaching adulthood. It is, however, important that by-standers realise that what looks like misbehaviour may have nothing to do with lack of discipline. A child who is hyperactive has a physical and intellectual problem which will not yield to smacks and threats. A child with autism may look angelic and behave diabolically! The cause of bizarre or disruptive behaviour does not reflect a failure of proper parenting. It is depressing for parents to be the butt of criticism rather than a focus of support and help. For them the incident is not isolated, although it may be the only one you see. It may be part of a cycle of difficulty from which there seems no escape, for which there is no help and about which no one seems available to care—except, maybe, *you*.

The other matter needing a brief mention is convulsions, fits. Epilepsy is fairly common among people with mental handicap and the prospect of needing to cope with a person having a fit is quite daunting. It is, however, a condition which is now well understood and people receiving regular medication may go for years without a fit. Where a person is liable to have fits, frequently the carer will inform and advise you on what to do if there is no one else around to cope. But don't panic—in all my years of involvement with hundreds of people with mental handicaps, I can count on one hand the number of times I have seen a person having a convulsion.

It is a natural tendency for us to want to protect people we see as vulnerable from the consequences of living in a hostile world. Protectionism is actually unhelpful. First, because it stops us listening to what people are behaving. (Sorry if that sounds dreadfully ungrammatical!) Second, because it makes them unduly dependent upon us rather than preparing them to cope with a wider range of human experience so that they learn to respond appropriately and are thus more widely welcomed into the community.

It's all too much

'People with handicaps receive a surfeit of goodwill but a deficit of practical help.'[2] We have shown that there are many ways in which practical help can be given. But that is, in itself, part of the problem! There are so many things to do, so many ways of tackling the issues, so much neglect to be reversed, for such a large number of people. Where shall we begin? Indeed, can we actually achieve anything worthwhile? What is the next thing to do?

Writing this miles from where you are, completely unaware of your situation and opportunities, and ignorant of the specific challenges you face, it would be presumptuous in the extreme if I were to attempt a blueprint approach to your unique set of circumstances. What I can do is offer a framework within which you can locate your response, and in such a way as to ensure that it is not just a pebble tossed in the sea, an isolated and insignificant act. The framework is one which now determines the response of A Cause for Concern to the challenges which the charity faces and by means of which it is encouraging churches to respond to the people in their districts or parishes who have mental handicaps. In practice that means that if you want to link in your response to that of others there is a way of doing so.

Stage 1: Friends—awareness and commitment

You at least are some way along the road to awareness of people with mental handicaps and their needs. Wouldn't it be good to have some fellow travellers! Start to get others to share your growing concern. Lend them this book. Better still buy them a copy (all the royalties go to charity). Talk to your minister and home group leaders. There is plenty of information available to help you.

Knowledge is, as we have seen, a forerunner to action. You cannot be aware of the neglect we have described without being moved to concern. As you talk with others about this your fire will warm their hearts too. Soon, maybe, you will want to talk and pray together about the people with mental handicaps in your church—or who are not in your church: the family in the congregation with a mentally handicapped child, or those you know in the locality. Out of your praying may come a personal or group commitment to people with mental handicaps. It is a reasonable expectation since God often creates a concern in us first, and then a commitment to do something in response to that concern. If that happens, when next?

Stage 2: Friends—spiritual ministry and integration

Recently I spent a pleasant hour at the dry ski slope in Llandudno, just as a spectator. It was fascinating to watch the variety of skiers on the slopes. Some were amazingly skilful, taking off from the very top, speeding over the hump half-way down and then weaving their way through the slower skiers to come to a stop in a flurry of white powder at the bottom. Near the end of the slope there was another entry point for skiers, for use by learners who came gingerly on to the run and moved forward with hesitant caution. How disastrous it would have been if the skier in the grey anorak had decided to trade his fragile confidence for a run from the top. Beware the same tendency in your response to people with mental handicaps.

Time and again I have heard from people with fantastic schemes to provide housing for people with mental handicaps, complete with estate agent's details of 'the ideal property'. To which I want to respond, 'And how will you pay for it?' Which may seem harsh in the light of my own experience, but it is usually enough to bring a touch of realism into the discussion. It's not that money is the problem but that the person has begun at the wrong place.

You don't have to wait until there are thousands of pounds in the bank or a property is on the market. A real response to people with mental handicaps can begin almost right away without having to find a penny! We can begin to offer them and their families one of the most precious commodities at our disposal—friendship. This will lay foundations on which to build significantly down through the years.

This is the point at which to begin to focus on real people. Having found out where they are (a process we have already considered), getting to know individuals is the next step. Perhaps this will be achieved by volunteering help to a club or society or family. These contacts can further nourish the concerns of the group meeting for prayer.

Sooner or later will come a concern to respond to the spiritual needs of the friends you make. It is unusual for one church to have sufficient people with mental handicaps attending to form a Bible group. Across several churches there may be six or more to form a core group for a regular meeting. All the information needed for setting up such a group is already available. (See *We're All Special to God*, Appendix 2.) Once it us under way the group can be the focus for attracting and involving other people with mental handicaps. It can begin to aid their acceptance and integration in their own churches.

One of the worries expressed by church leaders relates to the possible clash of Christian cultures that can result from this sort of meeting. Will it serve to confuse those who attend? Will it cause embarrassment in their home congregation? One of the few things common to people with mental handicaps is that their ability to generalise is limited. What happens in one setting is not readily transferable to a different setting. What they are used to in one church will not be expected to happen in a church of a different culture.

Once they become Christians it is important that people with mental handicaps are accepted as equal members within their own church. Helping this happen may fall to one of the leaders of the Bible group. Integration may prove quite a challenge to the way a church is used to doing things. Baptists may want a spoken testimony of conversion before they will recognise a person to be a Christian, which presents a problem to someone with no speech. Anglicans may want assent to the Apostles Creed from someone who cannot read. And so on. There may also be need for patience in dealing with inappropriate participation. The church may have to learn to listen carefully to receive 'ministry' from an unlikely source.

Stage 3: Friends—a network of practical support

This stage may be reached eventually, but not quickly. Those involved with people with mental handicaps will have grown in their appreciation of the issues which face their friends. They will know about their lifestyle, how they spend their days, the age and state of health of their parents, the problems arising from inadequate local resources.

It is likely that some common themes will begin to develop. It is also possible that meeting those needs can continue to be at relatively low cost. Let's look at some issues that tend to recur.

—Elderly parents find that increasing frailty causes practical difficulties. These may be a daily worry, like bathing a heavy son who cannot bath himself. Or they may struggle with the fact that they no longer can cope with holidays. The group might organise a holiday for some of their number. Or they might provide a family support project offering short-term care or practical assistance on a regular basis.

—Several of the group could live more independently if some way could be found of providing them with practical support. Accommodation might be found through a housing association or local authority if only a support worker could be organised. A local group might consider taking on such a project and 'managing' one of their number funded by the local authority.

—Local churches might consider funding someone to co-ordinate responses to the spiritual needs of people with mental handicaps in the wider area.

—As noted several times, day services may be in short supply. Some scheme to meet this without the need to buy buildings or invest heavily should be possible. Think of the number of underused church halls there must be in Britain!

These are just some of the ideas which spring to mind. Diversity of need offers enormously diverse opportunities to meet the needs. Many of the above may require the support of an organisation with professional expertise, the power to employ people, the skill to negotiate with local authorities. There are Christian groups available to help in these ways. As well as this there is need 'on the ground' for a little holy imagination, flair, faith and prayer to generate help for people with mental handicaps. It is of the essence of friendship to want to be helpful for the other person's benefit.

Stage 4: Friends—a full-time partnership

The group is probably now a few years down the road from where it began and in effective contact with local church leaders and a charity enabling local responses. And it is possible that the longer term need of a home beyond that which the parents can provide is now more apparent for at least some of the group.

At first glance the solution may look obvious—a residential care home. That may be the case, but not necessarily so. For example, adult placement may be an option. By this arrangement a person with a mental handicap lives with others of a similar age who may or may not form a family unit. Obviously the suitability of the people involved must be established, as must the long-term implications of the arrangement. But we must not expect more of the relationship than we expect of the home. It can and does work for many people. For Christians operating within a network of friends, it has potential to be a tremendously effective form of care. And with little capital cost.

Although this is still a relatively novel form of care it has enormous practical—and Christian—advantages. It can offer a secure ongoing home on the basis of 'life-sharing' between friends, one of whom happens to have a mental handicap. In the day-to-day experience of living with (more or less) non-handicapped peers the person with a handicap learns new skills, increases his vocabulary, grows in self-confidence, and more. He is thus more able to function in a socially acceptable manner at church and elsewhere. Such a scheme requires the support of others. The 'host' family or friends will face considerable demands on their time and energy. But how much more like the sharing of the early church, and what a powerful testimony to Christian love it provides!

To care for a group of people with mental handicaps is more expensive. Property has to be bought and adapted to meet regulations. If there are four or more residents those regulations are more extensive and demanding, including fire precautions. But the size of the group need not be large and the property can be quite ordinary. Again, co-operation with a charity already involved can achieve vastly more than trying to do everything from scratch.

Four stages towards meeting need! Within these broad bands all sorts of opportunities will present themselves. It must be obvious that there is much that can be done almost right away, without the need for extensive organisation or substantial sums of money.

It wants only the heart to be a friend

What will you do now that you have nearly finished this book? Within the suggestions made there must be something relevant to your particular situation. There may still be a need to review your attitudes and to practise thinking in a new and unaccustomed way about people with mental handicaps. But, without doubt, the best aid to positive attitudes is to get to know people affected in one way or another by the variety of conditions we lump together under one label. Then, perhaps, we will find that the labels are redundant! As our lives touch one another we shall wonder how we ever came to see mental handicap as a problem and why we thought of 'them' as having something wrong.

Notes

[1] F. Young, *Face to Face* (T & T Clark: Edinburgh, 1991), p 179.
[2] K.A. Rowlands, *Mental Handicap: Challenge to the Church* (Lisieux Hall: UK, 1991), p 129.

Conclusion

Now it's over to you. It feels as though I have poured myself out into what I have written. I hardly know what to say as I conclude. I hope that having read this book you will, somehow, never be the same again.

As I have written I have had in mind those to whom I owe so much. First, I've thought a good deal about how God feels on this issue. I dare to think that I have caught a glimpse of his concern. I hope you have too.

Second, I've thought about the people who have urged me on as I have been writing. Madeleine has been an inspiration, refreshing my own thinking with her own remarkable insight into the lives of people with mental handicaps. Peter Oakes has been another, enlarging my horizon immensely and challenging me to see what was before my eyes. Co-workers in A Cause for Concern have taken on extra work to give me space to write. I have tried to represent the shared passion of these colleagues that you might discover a fresh concern for people with mental handicaps.

Third, I have had constantly in mind my numerous friends who have mental handicaps. They are as mixed a bunch of friends as any. And it is quite normal that one wants others to accept one's friends. This has been my ambition for them— that you should accept them as your friends too. I have wanted to show off my friends, not so as to evoke your pity but to provoke your love.

There is a sense in which I don't want to let you go. I want to be reassured that you will do something for the friends of my friends. I want to know that you will stop putting them into conveniently labelled pigeon-holes. I want to feel that you will look beyond what may at first be unattractive. I want some evidence that you will give them space in your circle, in your church.

But I must let you go. You have been patient long enough. As you turn to face people who may be underdeveloped in their understanding, bent or buckled in their body, try to look beyond the disability to the person before you. 'The way you look at people can transform them.'[1]

There is something wrong when disabilities and handicaps exclude others from our company, deprive them of our love and shut them out from God's family. Please do something to put that right. For God's sake and theirs.

Note

[1] J. Vanier, *Man and Woman He Made Them* (Darton, Longman & Todd: London, 1985), p 5.

Appendix 1: Books

In recent years a significant number of books has been published on topics relating to mental handicap from both Christian and non-Christian perspectives. They tend either to be primarily biographical or largely technical, based on research findings. The books listed below are divided into three categories so that you can take a progressive look at reading round the subject. I have resisted the temptation to grade them with varying degrees of recommendation as the basis for that would be largely subjective. Some I would want to challenge at a number of points, particularly on matters of theology.

1 Reading for interest

Bowers, Faith. *Who's This Sitting In My Pew?*. Triangle/SPCK: London, 1988.

Bowers, Faith (ed). *Let Love Be Genuine: Mental handicap and the church*. Baptist Union of Great Britain: London, 1985.

Burton-Jones, Julia. *Caring For Carers* Scripture Union: London, 1992.

Davis, Alison. *From Where I Sit*. Triangle/SPCK: London, 1989.

Eden, Martyn, Potter, David and Thompson, Terry. *No Handicaps Please, We're Christians: The challenge of disability*. Causeway, 1990.

Hollins, Sheila, *When Mum Died*, and *When Dad Died*. Sovereign, St Georges Hospital Medical School: London.

Horwood, William. *Skallagrigg*. Penguin: London, 1988.

Lovell, Ann. *Simple Simon*. Lion: Tring, 1978.

MENTAL HANDICAP: IS ANYTHING WRONG?

Menniss, Una. *Special Children, Special God*. Kingsway: Eastbourne, 1990.

Morgan, Hazel. *Through Peter's Eyes*. Arthur James: London, 1990.

Nolan, Christopher. *Under the Eye of the Clock*. Pan: London, 1988.

Oswin, Maureen. *Am I Allowed to Cry?*. Souvenir Press: London, 1991.

Philps, Caroline. *Elizabeth Joy*. Lion: Tring, 1984.

Philps, Caroline. *Mummy, Why Have I Got Down's Syndrome?*. Lion: Oxford, 1991.

Potter, David. *Too Soon To Die*. Evangelical Press: Welwyn, 1982.

Spink, Kathryn. *Jean Vanier and L'Arche*. Darton, Longman & Todd: London, 1990.

Young, Frances. *Face To Face*. T & T Clark: Edinburgh, 1991.

What Everyone Should Know About Mental Handicap. (Scriptographic.) Causeway, 1990.

2 Reading for information

Brotchie, Jane. *Help At Hand: The Home Carers' Survival Guide*. Bedford Square Press: London, 1990.

Clifford, Sister Stephanie. *Called To Belong: Preparing mentally handicapped people for Confirmation*. Kevin Mayhew Pubishers: Bury St Edmunds, 1984.

Hubert, Jane. *Home-bound*. King's Fund Centre, 1991.

Leighton, Alan (ed). *Mental Handicap in the Community*. Woodhead-Faulkner: Cambridge, 1991.

McCloughry, Roy. *The Eye of the Needle*. Inter-Varsity Press, Leicester, 1990.

Powell, John. *Abortion: The Silent Holocaust*. Argus Communications: USA, 1981.

Ryan, Joanna, and Thomas, Frank. *The Politics of Mental Handicap*. Revised edition. Free Association Books: London, 1991.

Senior, Robert. *Towards a Better Understanding*. Euromonitor: London, 1985.

Schaeffer, Francis, and Koop, C. Everett. *Whatever Happened to the Human Race?*. Marshall, Morgan & Scott: Basingstoke, 1980.

Shaw, Ian. *Christian Family Matters*. Evangelical Press of Wales: Bridgend, 1985.

Stratford, Brian. *Down's Syndrome: Past, present and future*. Penguin: London, 1989.

Vanier, Jean. *Man and Woman He Made Them*. Darton, Longman & Todd: London, 1986.

Winter, Richard. *Choose Life*. Marshall, Morgan & Scott: Basingstoke, 1988.

3 Reading for instruction

Autton, Norman. *Touch: An Exploration*. Darton, Longman & Todd: London, 1989.

Barton, Len and Tomlinson, Sally (eds). *Special Education: Policy, practices and social issues*. Harper & Row: London, 1981.

Bowers, Faith, Robertson, Ena, and Wright, Susan. *Discipleship Booklets: Following Jesus; The Church; Joining the Church*. Baptist Union of Great Britain: London, 1991.

Brechin, Ann, and Swain, John. *Changing Relationships: Shared Action Planning with people with mental handicaps*. Harper & Row: London, 1987.

Carson, Herbert M. *Facing Suffering*. Evangelical Press: Welwyn, 1978.

Craft, Michael, Bicknell, Joan, and Hollins, Sheila (eds). *Mental Handicap: A multi-disciplinary approach*. Balliere Tindall: London, 1985.

Hollins, Sheila, and Grimer, Margaret. *Going Somewhere: People with mental handicaps and their pastoral care*. SPCK: London, 1988.

Kelly, Brian, and McGinley, Patrick (eds). *Mental Handicap: Challenge to the Church*. Lisieux Hall, 1991.

Kimpton, Diana, *A Special Child in the Family: Living with your sick or disabled child*. Sheldon Press: London, 1990.

Stewart Van Leeuwen, Mary. *The Person in Psychology*. Inter-Varsity Press: Leicester, 1985.

Stott, John. *Issues Facing Christians Today*. Marshalls: London, 1991.

Wenham, John. *The Goodness of God*. Inter-Varsity Press: Leicester, 1974.

Yule, William, and Carr, Janet (eds). *Behaviour Modification for People with Mental Handicaps*. Croom Helm: London, 1980.

4 Official Documents

The White Paper: *Caring For People. Community care in the next decade and beyond*. HMSO, 1989.

Home Life: A Code of Practice for Residential Care. Centre for Policy on Ageing, 1984.

Making a Reality of Community Care. Audit Commission. HMSO, 1986.

Mentally Incapacitated Adults and Decision Making. The Law Commission. HMSO, 1991.

Residential Care: A Positive Choice. Lady G.E. Wagner. HMSO, 1988.

In the event of difficulty in obtaining any of the above books, Royal MENCAP Bookshop may be able to assist. The address is 123 Golden Lane, London, EC1Y 0RT; telephone 071–454 0454.

Appendix 2: Resources

1 General resources

There are now more and more resources becoming available to help both people with mental handicaps and those wishing to assist them. This is a welcome development, but it means that by the time this list is published it will be overtaken by further publications.

Leisure Resource Pack from Mencap PRMH Project. A training pack for people with profound and multiple disabilities, enabling them to enjoy more meaningful leisure time. Apart from some 'New Age' material it is full of useful information and ideas.

Mental Handicap: Patterns For Living. Open University course P555. A useful basic training about mental handicap.

Patterns For Living: Working Together. Another Open University course (P555M), sequel to the above, for use with people who have mental handicaps.

Read Easy is a book of reading resources for adults with a mental handicap published by J. Whitaker and the Book Trust.

Videos: *Bill*, and *Bill On His Own* by Guild and Oddysey respectively. True story of a mentally handicapped man living in the community after decades in an institution. Leading part brilliantly portrayed by Mickey Rooney.

2 Christian resources

As noted in Chapter 5, several denominations are now seeking to provide relevant resources for their member churches in respect of mental handicap. Addresses for full information should be sought from denominational headquarters.

Causeway has developed several resources to create awareness and to enable Christians to be active in responding to people with mental handicaps. It is continually adding to its list of resources. Principal items include the following:

Christian Awareness Pack: Mental Handicap for individual or small group study.

Do It Yourself Training Pack: *The Local Church and Mental Handicap*, designed for training groups to become practically involved.

We're All Special to God by David and Madeleine Potter. This book explains how to set up and run a Bible group for people with mental handicaps, and includes material for nine sessions. Supplements are available from Causeway.

Causeway Training Video, providing training for setting up and running Bible groups.

The *Holy Bible* and the *New Testament* in the Easy to Read Version. A clear and simplified translation of the Bible ideally suited for use with people with mental handicaps.

The Father Himself Loves You, a cassette tape of songs written for use in worship by people with mental handicaps. A song book is also available.

Beautiful . . . or What?!, a unique album of music by Adrian Snell on the theme of mental handicap, published by Word (UK). A moving and penetrating musical play about the experience of a person with a mental handicap.

Appendix 3: Organisations

There are many voluntary organisations working among and for people with mental handicaps and their carers. With the development of community care there are also many private organisations providing services of various sorts. They require a directory rather than an appendix. Those listed will give you a way into the range of groups active in this field.

1 Organisations mentioned in this book

A Cause For Concern and **Causeway**, PO Box 351, Reading RG1 7AL

ARK Housing Association, The Priory, Canaan Lane, Edinburgh EH10

BUILD, 12 Barford Crescent, King's Norton, Birmingham B38 0BH

The Church of Scotland, Board of Social Responsibility, Wallace House, 3 Boswall Road, Edinburgh EH5 3RJ

The Church of Scotland, Education Department, One in a Hundred, 121 George Street, Edinburgh EH2 4YN

L'Arche, 14 London Road, Beccles, Suffolk NR34 9NH

The Lodge Trust, The Lodge, Market Overton, Oakham, Leics LE15 7PL

Moorfield House, Giddygate Lane, Melling, Merseyside L31 1AQ

St Joseph's Centre, The Burroughs, Hendon, London NW4 4TY

The Shaftesbury Society, 18–20 Kingston Road, London SW19 1JZ

Walsingham Community Homes, 2 Chester House, Pages Lane, London N10 1PR

2 Organisations which inform and support

ARC (Association for Residential Care), The Old Rectory, Church Lane North, Old Whittington, Chesterfield S41 9QY

ARC is an association of organisations and individual units providing residential and day services for people with mental handicaps. It also runs training courses and operates a National Vocational Qualification consortium.

CARE Trust (Christian Action, Research and Education), 53 Romney Street, London SW1P 3RF

CARE is an evangelical organisation expressing concern on a range of social and political issues.

CARESEARCH, c/o Janet Hepburn, Fairways, The Hudnalls, St Briavells, Lydney, Glos GL15 6SJ

CARESEARCH is a service of ARC maintaining a computerised record of provision of residential care homes and vacancies for people with mental handicaps.

CHAD (Church Action on Disability), Rev J. Pierce, Charisma Cottage, Drewsteignton, Exeter EX6 6QR

Encouraging and resourcing churches to be more aware of the need to be accessible, in every respect, to people with disabilities of any sort.

Down's Syndrome Association, 12–13 Clapham Common South Side, London SW4 7AA

A support organisation with local branches.

National Autistic Society, 276 Willesden Lane, London NW2 5RB

Support organisation with regional branches and some residential services.

RADAR (Royal Association for Disability and Rehabilitation), 25 Mortimer Street, London W1N 8AB

Main source of information on matters relating to physical disability.

Royal MENCAP, 123 Golden Lane, London EC1 0RT

Range of services including support of parent groups nationally and Gateway clubs for adults and young people with mental handicaps.

Caring For The Carers

by Christine Ledger

Caring means energy. It is not surprising, therefore, that long-term caring can become a physical and emotional assault-course for even the most compassionate person.

We can help those who look after others on a non-professional basis. Here some of them tell their own stories, before Christine Ledger—a carer herself both professionally and at home—goes on to suggest simple, realistic ways in which support and encouragement can be given to the unsung heroes of our society.

'An excellent, moving, practical, down-to-earth resource book for all those who are in the front line caring for family or friends, and for those who support them.'

DR PATRICK DIXON
Specialist in care of the dying and
Director, AIDS Care Education and Training

'A book that ought to be on every minister's shelves and in the home of any person who might one day find herself or himself at the point when caring passes into that area where they feel alone and forgotten.'
From the Foreword by **DR GEORGE CAREY**
Archbishop of Canterbury

This is part of a series of books published in association with CARE Trust, addressing the issues that call for political action and compassionate involvement and care.

 Kingsway Publications

Schizophrenia: Voices In The Dark

by Mary Moate & Dr David Enoch

Schizophrenia is everyone's concern. It affects 1 in 100 people in their lifetime. Every year there are 6,000 new cases in Britain alone. This disease does not discriminate between sexes, cultures, societies, faiths or professions.

This book is for those who care for the mentally ill in families, churches and a wider community.

Mrs Mary Moate is the mother of Philip, a schizophrenic child whose story is so movingly told here. A member of the Salvation Army, she is a voluntary community worker.

Dr David Enoch is a leading Consultant Psychiatrist and Special Advisor to Mersey Regional Health Authority. He is author of *Healing the Hurt Mind*.

Revd Dr Nigel M de S Cameron, Care Series Editor, is Theological Research Consultant to CARE, Warden of Rutherford House in Edinburgh, and Editor of *Ethics and Medicine*. He travels internationally to speak on theology and ethics.

This is part of a series of books published in association with CARE Trust, addressing the issues that call for political action and compassionate involvement and care.

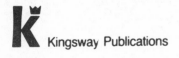

Kingsway Publications